STUDIES IN EASTERN CHRISTIANITY

Volume One

By the same author :

De magisterio ordinario Summi Pontificis (Toronto, 1966).

Українська церква – її сучасне й майбутнє (Торонто–Чікаґо, 1966).

За самопроголошення Українського Києво-Галицького Патріярхату (Торонто–Чікаґо, 1970).

Вибір єпископів в Українській Церкві (Торонто–Чікаґо, 1971).

Патріярхальний устрій помісної (particularis) Української Католицької Церкви. Текст і коментар (Торонто, 1974).

The Fifth Lateran Council (1512-1517) and the Eastern Churches (Toronto, 1975).

Торонто   1977

Printed in Canada

Printed by: PRUT Printing Co. Ltd., 241 Niagara St., Toronto, Ont., Tel.: 363-4640

THE UKRAINIAN FREE UNIVERSITY

Series: Monographs No. 25

studies

in

eastern christianity
volume one

by

PETRO B. T. BILANIUK

Munich — Toronto 1977

— III —

EPARCHY OF TORONTO
No. 14/77   February 4, 1977.

Imprimatur.

† *Isidore Borecky*
Eparch of Toronto

Distributed by the author:
Petro B.T. Bilaniuk
41 Parkway Avenue
Toronto, Ontario, Canada
M6R 1T6

ISBN 0-920322-00-X

to
the Right Reverend

Michael Schmaus

domestic prelate of his holiness
doctor and professor of theology
my esteemed teacher & adviser

on the occasion of his

eightieth birthday

1897 - July - 1977

acknowledgements:

The author's first expression of gratitude is hereby extended to the *Rector Magnificus* of the Ukrainian Free University in Munich, Professor Wolodymyr Janiw, Ph.D., who has graciously consented to write the foreword to this volume. Likewise, grateful acknowledgement is due to the Ukrainian Free University for undertaking this publication.

Further thankful acknowledgements are due to the various original publishers of the articles included in this collection for granting their kind permission to reproduce them here.

The author also wishes to express his sincere thanks to the following: Ewhen Chorostil, caligrapher and artistic designer; Michelle Marie Jennings and Mark Lodico compilers of the index; Isabel Massey and Yakiw Krekhovetsky, who assisted in editorial work, and H.Holowaty, printer.

Finally, the author wishes to thank his charming wife, Dr. F. Marie-Therese Bilaniuk, for her persevering patience and assistance during the course of his academic career.

The illustration on the title page is Olexa Povstenko's reconstruction of the West façade of St. Michael's Basilica in Kiev (constructed in 1108), taken from *Zolotoverkhyi Kyïv* – *Gold Topped Kiev*, No. 2, Washington, D.C. (n.d. /1954?/), p. 64. The icons reproduced on pages 1, 43, 69, 97 and 155 are taken from the Byzantine Ukrainian liturgical book *Chasoslov* (Rome, 1950). The original illustrations on pages 15 and 141 are the work of Ewhen A. Chorostil.

Easter 1977.   Petro B. T. Bilaniuk

fOREWORD:

The Ukrainian Free University was founded in 1921 in Vienna, Austria, and transferred in the fall of the same year to Prague, Czechoslovakia, where it received the support of that state and recognition of the scholarly world. After the disruption of World War II the University reopened in the fall of 1945 in Munich, Germany, under extremely difficult circumstances. On September 16, 1950 the Ukrainian Free University was officially recognized by the Bavarian Government and granted Charter No. XI 60710, by which all diplomas and academic degrees were given an official status and international academic recognition. During its existence as the only university in exile, the Ukrainian Free University has conferred a whole series of major academic degrees and issued some 160 volumes of scholarly works. By this contribution our university has served well the free scholarship and culture of humankind.

The author of this collection, Petro Borys Tereshkowych Bilaniuk, rich in the languages and culture of Ukraine and of all Europe, immersed in the classical and theological heritage of Christianity both East and West, was born in Zalishchyky, Ukraine, on August 4, 1932. After an 'Odyssey' through many countries, he came to Canada in September of 1949 and became a Canadian citizen on May 30, 1955. As his contribution to Ukrainian scholarship and to his new country, he obtained a Doctorate in Theology with *magna cum laude* from the University of Munich in 1961, and another Doctorate in Philosophy with *summa cum laude* from the Ukrainian Free University in 1972. Since 1962 Dr. Bilaniuk has pursued his honourable career as a professor of Theology and Religious Studies at the University of St. Michael's College in Toronto and the University of Toronto. In 1973 he also became a visiting professor of Church History at the Ukrainian Free University in Munich.

The Ukrainian Free University is proud to present the first volume of Professor Petro B.T. Bilaniuk's collected essays in English; it represents a series of diverse perspectives and interests of the author. Their common point of departure is the Eastern Christian spiritual optimism and *Weltanschauung,* which are firmly rooted in the pneumatic understanding of Sacred Scripture, the rich patristic and liturgical tradition, and rich in the live perception of the mysteries of the Christian faith and of the contemporary Christianity.

The ambient of these studies covers issues ranging from practical concerns of Christian life to ecclesiastical discipline, liturgical theology, philosophical and theological speculation, also questions pertaining to ecclesiastical history. The author uses the critical scholarly method both in his historical investigations and theological elaborations. These investigations are based on extensive and thorough academic research, and their themes engage him in the on-going dialogue of thinkers of both Eastern and Western Christian traditions. Previous to this volume, the author has also written on various theological and Church-historical subjects in Ukrainian, Latin, German and English.

The first work of the present volume is on prayer. It gives the foundation of a theological discussion concerning the intimate nature of prayer, based on Sacred Scripture and Origen, and it attempts to correct the one-sided description of prayer, which dominated Christian tradition ever since the writings of Euagrios Pontikos in the fourth century. The author describes prayer as a charisma of the Triadic God, a polylogue, and an ontological relationship. Here the author exhibits his uncompromising theocentric and anti-Pelagian orientation.

In his article on Transfiguration, we see an example of Eastern Christian liturgical theology elaborated as a theological theme encompassing the whole field of religious thought. This article is a classical example of what can be done with the incredibly rich and profound liturgical texts of the Eastern Churches.

Another central theme of Eastern Christian theology is the mystery of *theosis* or divinization. The author offers an introductory article to this extremely important theme which clearly distinguishes Eastern Christian theology from Western theology of grace.

One might wonder why an article on the Christology of Teilhard de Chardin is included in this volume dealing with Eastern Christianity. There is no doubt that Teilhard de Chardin was raised and educated in the Western Christian tradition. However, he constantly invokes the authority of the Eastern Fathers of the Church. This constitutes a major breakthrough, and is in fact an Eastern Christian mode of thought cast into a mould of evolutive *Weltanschauung*. Furthermore, the author of this volume, in analyzing Teilhard de Chardin, exhibits his Eastern Christian approach to this contemporary thinker.

'Celibacy and Eastern Tradition' is the longest investigation in this collection. It establishes the author as a very solid Church historian and researcher of the development of Christian thought and discipline This article is very well documented and based on original sources. However, the author does not stop there. In the last part he boldly criticizes both Eastern and Western traditions and advances concrete proposals for a re-examination of contemporary thinking and discipline on celibacy and the married priesthood.

For the last two hundred years Hryhorij Skovoroda has been considered as the greatest Ukrainian philosopher and one of the greatest minds in Eastern Europe. Professor Bilaniuk challanges the all too narrow identification of Skovoroda as a philosopher and proposes the view that he was primarily a theologian firmly rooted in Sacred Scripture and and the Eastern Patristic tradition. The evidence brought forth to support this view is very substantial.

In the last article the author analyses the Ukrainian Catholic lay movement in the light of an ethnopsychology of the Ukrainian people, an academic expertise which he developed under the guidance of the professorial staff of the Ukrainian Free University during his doctoral studies. There is no doubt that his analysis will provoke academic discussion which will be welcomed in the future.

In order to limit prohibitive expenditures of this publication it was decided to adopt the method of offset reproduction of the articles as they were originally published. This method does not permit renewed editing, i.e. the inclusion of desired corrections, or some omissions, and constitutes an evident drawback. However, we felt very strongly that these studies should be collected under one cover and offered to the scholarly community at large. We hope that this valuable collection will constitute a modest contribution to the inter-Christian dialogue and ecumenical endeavors of our day. In the spirit of the Second Vatican Council we trust that this volume will stimulate Eastern Christians to rediscover their rich spiritual heritage and share it with the rest of the world.

Prof. Wolodymyr Janiw, Ph.D.,

Rector

March 6, 1977

UKRAINIAN FREE UNIVERSITY
Pienzenauerstrasse 15
D-8000 München 80
West Germany

SOME REMARKS CONCERNING A THEOLOGICAL DESCRIPTION OF PRAYER

Originally published in *The Greek Orthodox Theological Review*, 21(1976), pp. 203–214; reprinted here with permission.

SOME REMARKS CONCERNING
A THEOLOGICAL DESCRIPTION OF PRAYER *

Literature concerning prayer is enormous. In fact, many of the most ancient written monuments are sacred or religious writings containing many different prayers, as well as views on the nature, importance, necessity, goal, usefulness and kinds of prayer.[1] Also, one normal human life would be by far too short to collect complete and scholarly bibliographical data concerning prayer in the Christian tradition alone. In recent times comparative-religious, ethnographical, ethnological, historical, philosophical, literary, psychological investigations, etc. of prayer are truly flourishing and bear many scholarly and scientific fruits.[2] However, in the area of Christian theological de-

---

* Sincere thanks are due to Mr. Yakiw Krekhovetskyi, who corrected the English of the manuscript. All biblical quotations are from the Revised Standard Version.

[1] Cf. T. Ohm, *Die Gebetsgebärden der Völker und das Christentum* (Leiden, 1948); P.W. Scheele, (ed.), *Opfer des Wortes. Gebete der Heiden aus fünf Jahrtausenden* (Paderborn, 1960).

[2] In the rich literature on prayer without doubt the most prominent place is occupied by F. Heiler, *Das Gebet. Eine religionsgeschichtliche und religionspsychologische Untersuchung* (Munich/Basle, 1969). Extensive bibliography is found on pp. 498-503 and 619-26. Translations of this work: *Prayer* (New York, 1932,1958); *La Priere* (Paris, 1931); *Bonen* (Stockholm, 1922). It is necessary here to mention another monumental work by the same author—a prominent scholar of the Christian East, *Die Ostkirchen* (Munich/Basle, 1971). There, on pp. 276-93, he deals with Eastern mysticism, hesychasm and prayer. On pp. 523-33 one finds an extensive bibliography. Among more recent works on prayer the most distinguished are: Th. Soiron, *Das Geheimnis des Gebetes* (Freiburg, 1937); J. C. Fenton, *The Theology of Prayer* (Milwaukee, 1939); V. Lossky, *Essai sur la théologie mystique de l'Eglise d'Orient* (Paris, 1944); Idem, *The Mystical Theology of the Eastern Church* (London, 1957); H. Kuhaupt, *Abba Vater. Christliche Lehre vom Gebet* (Freiburg, 1948); E. Behr-Siegel, *Prière et sainteté dans l'Eglise russe* (Paris, 1950); J. Arintero, *Grados de oracion* (Salamanca, 1950); J. de Monteleon, *Traité sur l'oraison* (Paris, 1950); H. Urs von Balthasar, *Das betrachtende Gebet* (Einsiedeln, 1955); R. Guardini, *Vorschule des Betens* (Einsiedeln, 1956); K. Rahner, *Von der Not und dem Segen des Gebetes* (Innsbruck, 1959); A. Hamman, *La Prière*. Vol. I. *Le Nouveau Testament* (Tournai, 1959); H. Urs von Balthasar, *Prayer*, tr. A. V. Littledale (New York, 1961); F. Wulf, *Gebet: Handbuch theologischer Grundbegriffe*, H. Fries, ed., (Munich, 1962) I,424-436; Φιλοκαλία τῶν ἱερῶν νηπτικῶν, 5 vols. Athens, 1963), Russian translation: *Dobrotoliubiie* (Moscow, 1905); an abbreviated English edition: *Writings from the Philokalia on Prayer of the Heart*, E. Kadloubovsky and G. E. H. Palmer, trans. (London, 1951); D. Z. Phillips, *The Concept of Prayer* (London, 1965); H. Dumoulin, *Östliche Meditation und christliche Mystik* (Freiburg/Munich, 1966);

scription of prayer one can notice a certain stagnation, for very few theologians and spiritual writers ventured beyond the definition of prayer given to us towards the end of the fourth century by Evagrios Pontikos in the 35th chapter of his famous *Chapters on Prayer*, which reads: "Prayer is an ascent of the spirit to God."[3]

It is not easy to explain why the Fathers of the Church and innumerable theologians have repeated either literally or with some more or less important additions precisely this definition of prayer, and why after one and a half millennia it still enjoys tremendous popularity. The above definition of prayer, which suggests a monologue originating in the human being, overshadowed other definitions and descriptions of prayer given by Evagrios Pontikos in his *Chapters on Prayer*, e.g. in chapter three we read: "Prayer is a continual intercourse of the spirit with God."[4] This definition quite clearly classifies prayer as a dialogue, and thus is much richer and more precise than the definition given in chapter thirty-five of the same work, which can be interpreted in a Pelagian sense, i.e. a human being can pray by his own power, on his own initiative and thus elicit supernatural acts of faith, hope, and love without divine assistance.

Thus it is clear that the definition of prayer contained in chapter 35 does not clearly indicate the efficient causality of prayer and can be interpreted as a purely human phenomenon which originates in the human being and which by the power of the same ascends to God. It is our intention to show that prayer is a supernatural act which is gratuitously given from above, or a charism of the Holy Spirit, i.e. it is a product of supernatural grace and originates within the realm of the primary or divine Causality. The divine and human synergism, which

---

J. von Gardner et al., *Kult und Kontemplation in Ost und West* (Regensburg, 1967); K. J. Healy, "Prayer, Theology of," *New Catholic Encyclopedia* (New York, 1967) 11.670-78; Ch. Humphreys, *Concentration and Meditation. A Manual of Mind Development* (London, 1968); Thomas Merton, *Contemplative Prayer* (New York, 1969); Idem, *The Climate of Monastic Prayer*(Spencer, 1969); K. Cragg,*Alive to God: Muslim and Christian Prayer* (London, 1970); O. H. Pesch, *Sprechender Glaube. Entwurf einer Theologie des Gebetes* (Mainz, 1970); Kirpal Singh, *Prayer: Its Nature and Technique* (Franklin, 1972).

[3] For the Greek text cf. PG 79:1173. For an English translation and a commentary cf. Evagrios Pontikos, *The Praktikos. Chapters on Prayer* (Spencer, Mass., 1970).

[4] Ibid., p. 56.

composes the act of prayer, does not detract from the above mentioned fact of the divine initiative and condescension. In this article we shall deal first of all with the concept of 'natural' prayer, which flows from the very core of our being. Further, we shall consider the witness of Holy Scripture concerning prayer as a supernatural reality, which is given to us along with the supernatural virtues of faith, hope and love, all of which constitute the supernatural foundation of prayer. Subsequently we shall define prayer not as a monologue, or a dialogue, but as polylogue, i.e. as a conversation and exchange of spiritual goods between three or more parties. Finally, on the basis of all previous expositions we shall try to give a theological description of prayer. We say a 'description' and not a 'definition,' simply because each true prayer (i.e. both Christian and non-Christian) is a mysterious reality in the order of action with very far-reaching consequences in the semantic, logical and ontological orders. Besides, each prayer reflects the cultural, spiritual, psychological, ethnopsychological, philosophical, religious forms, heritage, etc. of the one who prays. For these reasons it is not possible to strictly define prayer. It is possible only to describe it more or less exactly.

In its primitive and fundamental form, prayer can be described as an act of cult by which a human being feels called to attempt to establish a contact, or in fact establishes one, with the highest, superhuman extrasensory being, which is believed to be a personal, true and truly present being, on whose omnipotent glory one feels dependent. Already this very general description of each true prayer points to the fact that each human person is a being destined for prayer. In the life of each of us there comes a moment during which we experience an inner necessity, or even an uncontrollable urge to know, love, and worship either some superhuman element, or the eternal, infinite, true, holy, omnipotent, and infinitely beautiful being from whom the whole human being totally depends in its life, existence, and activity. The same phenomenon can be observed on the social level when some human society starts to experience a desire for a communal religious expression and for public cult. This state and activity was very well described by Tertullian's famous statement *anima naturaliter Christiana* (a soul is naturally Christian).[5] This means that a human being possesses an inborn tendency and capacity to know, love, and worship God, for a human being is naturally open to an eventual divine self-revelation, and precisely this prepares and predisposes him to reception of the Christian faith. Therefore, a Christian concept of prayer on the one hand must be based precisely on this natural, intrinsic, and God-given structure of the human being, who is a rational, social, emotional, sexual, esthetic, economic, and religious being. On the other hand the reality of Christian prayer must be rooted in the divine and divinizing process (in Greek *theosis*, in Latin *divinisatio*), into which a human being is drawn by a call of the Triadic God and invited to respond to Him freely in faith, hope, and love.

Here we have to beware of a possible misunderstanding which would interpret *theosis* or divinization as a true 'deification,' or a transformation of the human being into 'god.' In this issue I made my position clear:

> Theosis or divinization (or sometimes even deification) can be described as the omnipotent and sanctifying, divine and Triadic activity which, because of the indwelling of the Trinity and grace, and because of the unborn and natural capacity of the creature for transfiguration, induces a process of assimilation to God the Father of the whole human person, of mankind and of the visible and invisible universe in its totality, through the mediation of the incarnate Logos, Christ the Pantocrator, and in the Holy Spirit.[6]

This tendency to divinization or even deification can be observed in many religions of the world. There is no doubt, that the human being has a natural tendency towards transcendence or self-transcendence towards the absolute, the infinite, and the eternal, which manifests itself in the religious phenomena of meditation, prayer, contemplation, cult, moral responsibility, tendency towards the holy, mysterious, and occult, etc.

---

5 Apol. 17.6: PL 1:377. Cf. on this topic also my article "Anima Naturaliter Christiania,"*New Catholic Encyclopedia*, 1.545.

6 P.B.T. Bilaniuk, "The Mystery of Theosis or Divinization," *The Heritage of the Early Church* [Florovsky, *Festchrift*]. D. Neiman and M. Schatkin (eds.), Orienfalia Christiana Analecta 195 (Rome, 1973), 337-59.

These phenomena must be interpreted primarily as a tendency towards divinization, or better, as a process of divinization which leads towards the eschatological fulfillment in a certain form of union with the Godhead. In my opinion, this constitutes a cornerstone of an interfaith polylogue on prayer, cooperation, and mutual understanding.

But let us return to the question concerning supernatural prayer, which is a call and a gift of the Triadic God, and which originates from his initiative. The Hebrew language of the Old Testament preserved many different terms which express prayer or cultic activities.[7] In the Old Testament we find also many descriptions of traditional elements of prayer, namely adoration, glorification, thanksgiving, and imploration. All Old Testament prayers and divine names are structured in such a way that they may be applied or directed to the one and unique God only, Whose name is Yahweh, or 'He who is,' i.e. whose essence is existence itself. Yahweh is the Creator of heaven and earth. He is the only ruler of the general history of the whole cosmos and of the special history of salvation. He is omnipotent and omnipresent, and therefore He can freely enter into a covenant with His chosen people Israel (Lev 26.1-46). And it is precisely He, Yahweh, who calls Israel to prayer and invites all its members to a prayerful dialogue. The vocation of Abraham by Yahweh (Gen 12.1-3) is a prototype of the divine initiative in establishing the official and private prayer, or spiritual dialogue. The most classical example of this call of Yahweh to a prayerful dialogue we find in Deut 6.4-9. This text proves that the supernatural prayer is not the doing of man, but of God, who calls man to prayer and transfigures him by His divine grace; and it is then, and only then, that the true prayer on the part of man becomes possible.[8]

Prayer as a dialogue originating from God's initiative is beautifully described in 1 Sam 3.10:

[7] For the biblical aspect of prayer cf. J. de Fraine, *Praying with the Bible*, tr. J. W. Saul (New York, 1964); M. R. E. Masterman, "Prayer in the Bible," *New Catholic Encyclopedia*, 11.669-70.

[8] On the mystery of Transfiguration of Christ, man, and the visible and the invisible cosmos see my article "A Theological Meditation on the Mystery of Transfiguration," *Diakonia* 8(1973)306-31.

And the Lord came and stood forth, calling as at other times, 'Samuel! Samuel!' And Samuel said: 'Speak, for thy servant hears.'

Concerning this prayerful dialogue and its rejection the prophet Jeremias (35.17) wrote:

Therefore, thus says the Lord, the God of hosts, the God of Israel: Behold, I am bringing on Judah and all the inhabitants of Jerusalem all the evil that I have pronounced against them; because I have spoken to them and they have not listened, I have called to them and they have not answered.

In the book of the prophet Isaias (50.2) Yahweh again expresses His displeasure:

Why, when I came, was there no man?
When I called, was there no one to answer?
Is my hand shortened, that it cannot redeem?
Or have I no power to deliver?
Behold, by my rebuke I dry up the sea,
I make the rivers a desert;
   their fish stink for lack of water,
   and die of thirst.

In the Old Testament there are many examples of Yahweh's dialogue with Israel, in which on Yahweh's initiative Israel praises Him for His uniqueness, glory, and omnipresence and thanks Him for His omnipotent assistance, His great deeds, and wonderful gifts. Also, Israel brought before Yahweh in its prayers all its troubles, needs and sorrow, for Yahweh was to Israel the personal God, the omnipotent Lord, and a friend in heaven.

Origen, who was the first Christian author to write a *Booklet on Prayer*, was aware of the above teaching concerning prayer:

The grace of God, immense and beyond measure, showered by Him on men through Jesus Christ, the minister to us of this superabundant grace, and through the co-operation of the Spirit, makes possible through His will things which are to our rational and mortal nature impossible. For they are very great, and beyond man's compass and far transcend our mortal condition. It is impossible, for example, for human nature to acquire wisdom by which all things were made (for according to David, God has made all things in wisdom); yet, from being impossible it becomes possible through Our Lord Jesus Christ . . ?[9]

A little further in ch. 2.6 of the same work Origen adds:

Since then to treat of prayer is such a great task that one needs for it the illumination of the Father, the instruction of the *first-born* Word Himself, and the operation of the Spirit, in order to understand and speak as one ought of such a problem, I beseech the Spirit—imploring Him as a man (for I myself make no claim whatever of being able to pray) before I begin to speak of prayer—that we may be given, to speak fully and spiritually and may explain the prayers recorded in the Gospels.[10]

No doubt, this is one of the most important texts concerning the nature of prayer, for it is presented here as a supernatural gift of the Triadic God, which comes from above and as a result of that carries upon itself a Triadic seal. Besides, this supernatural charisma or gift called prayer is very clearly distinguished from mere human and natural activity, which is described as beseeching or imploring. However, Origen's concept of prayer was unfortunately overshadowed since the end of the fourth century by the definition of prayer of Evagrios Pontikos mentioned above.

Prayer by its very nature is a *polylogue*. It is not a monologue of one person or another who does not answer or maybe does not even listen. It is not a dialogue, or a conversation of two persons exchanging ideas and spiritual goods. Prayer is an interpersonal polylogue because it necessarily involves many persons. It is necessarily a call of God the Father, through the Son, and in the Holy Spirit, to man, woman, child, but as a member of the whole human community. Prayer is also an answer of man, woman, or a child, who are members of the

[9] Origen, *Prayer: Exhortation to Martyrdom*, tr. and annotated by J. J. O'Meara (Westminster, 1954), p. 15.

[10] Ibid., p. 21.

human community, which is generated by the natural and supernatural experience, activity, and events of their existence.

In the inner divine life of the Most Holy Trinity we see the prayer of God the Son to God the Father and in the Holy Spirit. There also we discover the prayer of the Holy Spirit through the Son to the Father on behalf of mankind and of the whole world. This divine prayer between the Three Divine Persons precedes and accompanies any prayerful human activity of an individual or of a society. The same divine prayer also fills in the gaps in human prayer, whenever it is imperfect on account of human weakness, or it even supplants our prayer whenever it is lacking on account of a physicial impossibility, as in the case of an infant or a mentally retarded person.

All we have just said is exemplified by Christ the Lord. In the New Testament we can observe a tremendous intensification of prayer, that is of a dialogue between God and a human being, as well as between God and the human community or mankind. Again, we see the divine initiative, for it is God the Father Himself Who in the Holy Spirit spoke into the world His Divine Word, His only-begotten Son, and the same Divine Word became flesh and dwelled among us. Through the mystery of Inhominization (a term I coined, for it is closer to the mysterious reality than 'Incarnation') the Divine Word became our brother and our Lord, for He assumed full human nature and a true historic existence, except sin. Our Lord and brother Jesus Christ offered to God the Father the most perfect prayerful answer, for in the name of the whole human race and of the whole cosmos He Himself in the Holy Spirit (i.e. in the divine atmosphere of light, life, and love) and in full obedience and as a perfect sacrifice returned in the mystery of His holy ascension to God the Father. This was the most perfect act of prayer, for it took place between God the Father and one of us—the New Adam—who at the same time was one of the Most Holy Trinity, i.e. the Son, the Divine Word and the Pneumatophor *par excellence,* i.e. the only true carrier of the Spirit.

When we take a closer look at the witness of the New Testament, we can observe that the prayer of Christ the Lord is primarily an act of listening to God the Father in order to perform a command of His Divine and salvific will. We see this in the life of Christ already at the age of twelve, when He decided to remain in the Temple. His answer to Joseph and to His blessed Mother is crystal clear: "How is it that you sought me? Did you not know that I must be in my Father's house?" Further regarding Christ's listening to the voice of His Father we read in the narrative about His stay in the desert after His baptism in the Jordan (Mk 1.12), and each time when on account of some event he suddenly felt that "his hour has come" (Jn 12.23;17.1), or that as yet it did not come (Jn 2.4). The Holy Gospel portrays Christ first of all as a listener (Jn 5.30). It cannot be otherwise, for He said of Himself (Jn 5.19,21):

> Truly, truly, I say to you, the Son can do nothing of his own accord, but only what he sees the Father doing; for whatever he does, that the Son does likewise . . . For the Father raises the dead and gives them life, so also the Son gives life to whom he will.

Each revelation of good news which Christ transmitted to mankind was given to Him beforehand by God the Father (Jn 17.8). Also each major decision made by Christ was preceded or accompanied by a prayer, which in fact was an act of listening to the voice of God the Father. We see this during His baptism in the Jordan and the unction with the Holy Spirit (Lk 3.21); before the vocation of the twelve Apostles (Lk 6.12); before His Transfiguration (Lk 9.28); before His Passion (Mt 26.36), etc. It is always God the Father Who in the Holy Spirit begins His prayerful conversation with His Son, the New Adam, Who answers in the name of the whole of mankind and of the whole cosmos. In the narrative concerning the Baptism of Christ in the Jordan (Lk 3.21 and Mt 17.5) we read of the open heaven, the voice of God and Father, and the descent of the Holy Spirit. All these events are the symbols of our salvation and sanctification as well as the fruits of the prayerful dialogue between the Father and the Son in the Holy Spirit. And precisely this is the foundation of describing prayer as a polylogue.

The polylogue character of prayer becomes manifest in the fact that the human being necessarily acts and prays as a member of the Church, of mankind, and of the created visible and invisible cosmos of which he, she, or it is a representative, even if this is not intended. The polylogue character of prayer is truly visible in the Divine Liturgy in which the bishop, priests, deacons, readers, and laity alternately express their prayerful views and feelings, all of which coalesce into one powerful drama. In this prayerful drama, through eucharistic *kenosis*, the Divine Inhominized Logos reveals Himself as the sacrificing High Priest, as the sacrificial victim and eucharistic food, and as the pantokratic Lord. The Holy Spirit through a *kenotic epi-klesis*,[11] is intimately connected with the polylogue drama, which evolves in front of and ascends to God the Father, and which makes His presence possible through the Son and in the Holy Spirit. This is so, because the Father is the Head of the Divine Family to which all persons and all things are called as to their ultimate end.

The pneumatic quality of Christian prayer is firmly rooted in the biblical witness. Therefore it is essentially a prayer in the Holy Spirit. This, however, is true of all aspects of spiritual life, for the Holy Spirit is the dynamic and moving power in the world.[12] St. Paul teaches (Rom 8.14-17):

> For all who are led by the Spirit of God are sons of God. For you did not receive the spirit of slavery to fall back into fear, but you have received the spirit of sonship. When we cry, "Abba! Father!" it is the Spirit himself bearing witness with our spirit that we are children of God, and if children, then heirs, heirs of God and fellow heirs with Christ, provided we suffer with him in order that we may also be glorified with him.

A little further on (Rom 8.26-27) St. Paul adds:

---

11 On the epiclesis cf. S. Khaburskyi, *Epikleza* (Yorkton, 1968) [in Urkrainian]; M. J. Giacchi, "Epiclesis," *New Catholic Encyclopedia*, 5:464-66(Bibl.).

12 For Eastern Christian doctrine concerning the role of the Holy Spirit cf. S. Boulgakof, *Le Paraclet*, trans. C. Andronikof (Paris, 1944); P. A. Florensky, "The Holy Spirit," *Ultimate Questions*, ed. A. Schmemann, (New York, 1965)137-73; T. Hopko, "Holy Spirit in Orthodox Theology and Life," *Commonweal*, 6(1968) 186-92; P. Evdokimoff, *L'Esprit Saint dans la tradition orthodoxe* (Paris, 1970); D. Staniloae, "The Role of the Holy Spirit in the Theology and Life of the Orthodox Church," *Diakonia* 9(1974)343-66.

Likewise the Spirit helps us in our weakness; for we do not know how to pray as we ought, but the Spirit himself intercedes for us with sighs too deep for words. And he who searches the hearts of men knows what is the mind of the Spirit, because the Spirit intercedes for the saints according to the will of God.

It is the Holy Spirit who gives us the prerequisites and fruits of real Christian prayer. He gives us knowledge and love (Eph 1.17f; 3.14-21; 2 Thess 3.5), peace and joy (Rom 15.33; Gal 5.22; 2 Thess 3.16) and, finally, unity (Rom 15.5). But His primary function is to be the Spirit of truth, who reminds us of Christ and His heavenly Father, and prompts us to witness and prayer (Jo 14.25-26; 15.26-27). The role of the Advocate in the Church and the world is very extensive and describes the context in which Christian prayer takes place (Jo 16.5-16). It is this gracious activity of the Holy Spirit which comes to us as a call, or as a warning, or as a strengthening, or as a consolation, or as an illumination of our minds. It comes to us to open our hearts, as a motion by which the listeners of the Word of God realize their sinful condition, and reverting from it, convert themselves to Christ with a prayerful contrition (Acts 2.40; 9.31; 11.22f; 13.15; 14.14; Rom 8.28-30; 12.8; 1Cor 14.3; 2 Cor 8.4; Heb 12.5; 1 Tim 4.13).

It is the Holy Spirit Who makes a human being capable to speak the faithful and prayerful 'Yes' to Jesus the Lord (1 Cor 12.13; 1 Jn 4.2-3; Eph 1.17-18). He gives to the human spirit an internal witness that he, the human being, is a child of God (Rom 8.16; 1 Jn 3.19-24). He also prays in the human being when he is silent before God (Rom. 8.26f; 1 Jn 2.20-27; Jn 16.13).

The awareness of this biblical teaching concerning the Holy Spirit and His activity is very vivid in Eastern Christianity. The best example, however, is a prayer to the Holy Spirit from Byzantine Liturgy:

Heavenly King, Consoler, the Spirit of Truth, present in all places and filling all things, the Treasury of blessings and the Giver of life: come and dwell in us, cleanse us of all stain and save our souls, O Good One! [13]

13 J. Raya-J. de Vinch (eds.), *Byzantine Daily Worship,* Allendale, N.J. 1969), p. 37.

214

Origen was aware of this pneumatological view of prayer when he wrote:

> Our understanding cannot pray if the Spirit has not, as it were in its hearing, prayed before it. In the same way it cannot sing nor hymn the Father in Christ with due rhythm and melody, time and harmony, unless *the Spirit* that *searcheth all things, yea, the deep things of God*, first has praised and hymned Him whose *deep things* He has searched and, as He is fully able, understood.[14]

In conclusion let me attempt to describe Christian prayer from an Eastern stance: Christian prayer is a mysterious and loving gift of God the Father through the Son and in the Holy Spirit, which comes to us as a supernatural call in faith, hope, and love, and develops into an intimate and personal polylogue with the Tri-Personal God, which includes His praises, petitions, and thanksgiving, and is the expression of a participation in His inner life, light, and love, and which ascends from us to God the Father, as to the Head of the Divine Family, through the Son and in the Holy Spirit.

[14] Origen, *Prayer*, p. 20, i.e., *Booklet on Prayer*, 2.4.

a theological meditation on the mystery of transfiguration

Originally published in *Diakonia. A quaterly devoted to advancing the Orthodox-Catholic dialogue*, 8(1973), pp.306-331. Reprinted here with permission.

A THEOLOGICAL MEDITATION ON THE MYSTERY OF TRANSFIGURATION

by Dr. Petro B. T. Bilaniuk

Prof. Bilaniuk teaches at the University of St. Michael's College in the University of Toronto. He is a Ukrainian Catholic long interested in presenting the treasures of Eastern Christianity to the West.

The pericope containing the narrative of the Transfiguration of our Lord is found in all three of the Synoptic Gospels, namely in Mk. 9,1-12; Mt. 17,1-13 and Lk. 9,28-36. The most primitive, and by the same token closest to the original oral catechesis, seems to be the account of Mark.

Unfortunately that beautiful account of the New Testament containing the very vivid and profound description of a theophany has not received sufficient theological attention in Western Christianity. However, it is true that there are some excellent exegetical works explaining either the historical and typological significance of this account or the examination and comparison of the parallel texts in the three Synoptics or the literary and stylistic composition, etc.[1] There are also some beautiful works dealing with the mystery of Transfiguration in art.[2] However, little or no strictly theological analysis of the mystery of the Transfiguration itself can be found in Western Christianity, e.g. in most of the Christological, ecclesiological, eschatological, etc. treatises there is no mention of the Transfiguration at all, and those works which contain some references to it offer usually less than the exegetical treatments.[3] The Second Vatican Council did not make any mention of the Transfiguration at all and there seem to be a few direct allusions to this mystery. And yet, we could have expected some modest reference to this mystery from an Ecumenical Council dealing with the renewal of the Church.

Also, during the Congress and Institute on the Theology of the Renewal of the Church marking the Centenary of Canada, which was held in Toronto August 20 to 25, 1967,[4] nobody seemed to mention the mystery of Transfiguration, even if the theology of the renewal of the Church would suggest a very intimate link between the two. My reaction was to take a direct stand during one of the panel discussions at the above mentioned Congress where among other things I stated:[5]

> My second remark . . . concerns the Transfiguration of our Lord recorded in Mark 9,1-7, Matt. 17,1-8, Luke 9,28-36. There is no adequate theology of the Transfiguration in the West. It is usually reduced to a proof of Christ's Divinity and to a didactic element in the preparation of the Apostles for Christ's Passion. According to Oriental theology, however, it was a revelation of a hidden supernatural reality, which is constantly present and constantly progressing in the Church and the cosmos. It is the supernatural 'dynamis' of God the Father, through the Son and in the Holy Spirit, which mystically and invisibly transforms, transfigures, sanctifies and fulfills the Church and the world, in preparation for the final fulfillment in the Kingdom of God.
>
> It is the doctrine of the spiritual optimism of the early Fathers of the Church who see the cosmos transfigured in God. Any real theology of renewal must take this aspect into account otherwise it will view the renewal as coming from below and not as the work of God or from above.

This quotation reflects the substance of my paper and will serve us as a guideline in our theological meditation.

While it is true that Eastern Christianity cannot match the quantity of literature on Transfiguration produced by Western Christianity, nevertheless Eastern Christianity developed and preserved a much greater awareness of this mystery in the concrete ecclesial life, in art, in theology and especially in liturgy.[6] During our meditation it will be our duty to quote the relevant passages of the Byzantine Liturgy dealing with the mystery of Transfiguration and to show their relevance to the theological interpretation of the same mystery.[7]

Extension of Transfiguration

First of all it seems that the mystery of Transfiguration has a much wider extension than is usually suspected. It affects in different degrees of intensity all parts of both the natural and the supernatural reality of which we are an integral part. As a matter of fact, already the correct description of any mystery of the Christian Faith presupposes such an extension as well as an interconnection with all other mysteries and this not only in a logical or semantic order but in the order of ontology or in the natural and supernatural reality as it exists in itself regardless of the consideration of our reason or the involvement of our will and feelings.

This is so because a mystery of the Christian Faith can be described as a living and life-giving, supernatural, divinely revealed reality, which is founded on the one hand on a historic fact and on the other hand on a permanent, dynamic and uninterrupted presence in the supernatural world. Thus any mystery of the Christian Faith on account of its dynamic quality has a transfiguratory dimension or effects.

Secondly we have to observe that the term transfiguration, which implies a natural or supernatural, visible or invisible (but always a dynamic) change of appearance, contents, state or relationship, is an analogical term which can be used in different contexts and with different intensities of meaning.

It seems that one of the most radical expressions of the mystery of Transfiguration can be seen in the divine act of creation, that is in the divine act of love which visits nothingness and transforms it or transfigures it into an existing reality. Thus this reality becomes an expression of God's love and a finite image of this infinite glory. This created reality, be it material or spiritual, natural or supernatural, visible or invisible, is by the very fact of its existence transfigurable, because of an inherent capacity rooted in its being for transfiguration or development and final fulfillment in the inner life and love of the Triadic God. Thus the *potentia oboedientialis* (i.e. potency of obedience) of each existent for the supernatural fulfillment or divinization should be expressed partly in terms of transfigurability or capacity to receive within itself the activity of the Transfigurer *par excellence* or God, who by His transcendent and immanent dynamism can intensify in a creature the expression of His glory.

The Byzantine Liturgy

These theological views concerning the nature of mystery in general and of the mystery of Transfiguration in particular are quite clearly expressed in the Byzantine Liturgy, i.e. in the hymns sung at Vespers at the lamp-lighting Psalms on the Feast of the Holy Transfiguration of Our Lord, God and Savior Jesus Christ:[8]

> Indeed, O Lord, the mountain that had been dark with smoke today becomes honorable and holy because You stood on it; the mystery hidden from the beginning of the world becomes manifest in Your Transfiguration before Peter, James and John, who fell with their faces to the ground, unable as they were to bear the light of Your countenance and the splendor of Your clothing. A further marvel was the vision of Moses and Elias conversing with You on Your future and the voice of the Father bearing witness and saying: "This is my beloved Son in whom I am well pleased. Hear Him. He is the One who will convey great mercy upon the world."

Again the *kontakion* in preparation of the Feast of Transfiguration reads:[9]

> Today the whole human race prepares to reflect the radiance of divine splendor brought about in the Transfiguration of Christ and to cry out with joy: "Christ is transfigured in order to save us all!"

The transfiguratory effects of the divine power are also beautifully described during the above mentioned Vespers:[10]

> O Lord, when You were transfigured before being crucified, Mount Thabor was made to resemble heaven, for a cloud was extended as a canopy and the Father bore witness to You.

In this cosmological context it is necessary to mention evolution and its relation to transfiguration. Here evolution is understood in terms of Teilhard de Chardin as the very law of the universe created in time-space continuum with the universe itself.[11] Thus evolution is not only a constant development but also a general ordering of all things under the pressure of the interval law and dynamics of the energetics of love. The concept of cosmic, biological and anthropological evolution clarifies before our bewildered eyes the concept of dynamic and progressing reality which tends to the hyperpersonal and transcendent Omega Point, that is the cosmic Christ and ultimately God. The foundation of this tendency is the law of complexity-consciousness which makes it possible for the evolving reality to tend with an irreversible direction towards the Omega Point. Thus evolution discloses reality as a creature in a constant natural process of transfiguration. This can be gathered from Teilhard's works, especially from two representative passages. The first one is taken from "Super-Humanité," Super-Christ, Super-Charité (1943):[12]

> In effect, since ultimately all things in the Universe are moved towards Christ the Omega; since all cosmogenesis, including anthropogenesis, is ultimately expressed in a Christogenesis; it follows that, in the integrity of its tangible layers, Reality is charged with a divine Presence. As the mystics sense and portray it, everything becomes physically and literally lovable in God; and reciprocally God becomes knowable and lovable in all that surrounds us. In the greatness and depths of its cosmic stuff, in the maddening number of elements and events which compose it, and in the fullness of the general currents which dominate and set it in motion like a great wave, the World, filled with God, no longer appears to our opened eyes as anything but a milieu and an object of universal communion.

The second passage is contained in "La vie cosmique" (March 24, 1916):[13]

> Since Jesus was born and grew to his full stature and died, everything has continued to move forward *because Christ is not yet fully formed:* he has not yet gathered about him the last folds of his robe of flesh and of love which is made up of his faithful followers. The mystical Christ has not yet attained to his full growth; and therefore the same is true of the cosmic Christ. Both of these are simultaneously in the state of being and of becoming; and it is from the prolongation of this process of becoming that all created activity ultimately springs. Christ is the end-point of the evolution, even the *natural* evolution, of all beings; and therefore evolution is holy.

One could object that Teilhard does not use the term "transfiguration" in the above mentioned texts. However, it is clear that the concept of both natural and supernatural transfiguration is indeed clearly indicated in these texts. Moreover, there are several texts in which Teilhard uses the terms "transfiguration," which prove that he was aware of the dynamic presence of this mystery in the surrounding reality. Thus speaking about "detachment through action" Teilhard reminds the readers of "Le Milieu

Divin," that "They should bear in mind that we are still only half-way along the road which leads to the mountain of the Transfiguration."[14] However, the most explicit teaching on Transfiguration in Teilhard can be found in his "Christ in the World of Matter"[15] in which he describes a mystic experience of one of his friends (actually his own), concerning the presence of Christ in the surrounding material world and God as "the Heart of Everything." There he uses such terms as transform, transfiguration, transfigure, transformation, and even the Greek term *metamorphosis*.

Scriptural Parallelism

With all this in mind, let us return to the account of the Transfiguration of Our Lord cited above. We read there, that "Jesus took Peter, James and John and led them up a high mountain" (Mk. 9,1). Now prayer or any event on a mountain in both Testaments means symbolically a very special presence of God. It establishes the link with the Old Testament and the divine theophany during the giving of the Law on the Mount Sinai (Ex. 24). In both cases this theophany takes place in the form of a cloud from which comes the voice of God. Both Jesus and Moses undergo a glorious transfiguration (Ex. 34,29f). The parallelism between Moses on Sinai and Jesus on Mount Thabor (according to Tradition) is therefore very strong in these as well as in some other points, e.g. Moses receives a command from God to take with him three men as official witnesses to the theophany, i.e. Aaron, Nadab, and Abiu (Ex. 24, 1-2). But what is the exact significance of the Transfiguration of our Lord on "a high mountain"? There are many aspects to this mystery and consequently many different answers can be given. However, the most important theological interpretation in my opinion is that the mystery of the Transfiguration of our Lord sums up the whole history of salvation and the structure of the supernaturalized or divinized cosmos.

In this context let me quote Michael Schmaus:[16]

God reveals Himself to man in a three-storey metaphysical-vertical and in the three-staged historico-salvational horizontal. He proclaims himself firstly in the three storeys of nature, spirit and Christ, as well as in the three stages, (that is) in the creation of the world, in the revelation in Christ, and in the fulfillment of the world. In Christ meet and cross the horizontal and the vertical. The first two metaphysical stages represent the 'natural' and Christ constitutes the 'supernatural' revelation of God. The latter does not build itself upon the first two stages of the natural revelation. Rather it penetrates and embraces them.

When we apply this evidently schematic and didactic teaching to the mystery of the Transfiguration of Our Lord, then we can discover that the presence of Moses constitutes the first horizontal stage, because he epitomizes the Old Testamental history of salvation starting with the creation of the world and ending with the coming of Christ. The second horizontal stage is the transfigured Jesus, who epitomizes the revelation of God made in Him starting with His conception and ending with the mission of the Spirit on the day of Pentecost. Elias, being an eschatological person *par excellence* in late Jewish apocalyptic literature, represents both the precursor of Jesus, i.e. John the Baptist, and along with Jesus the history of salvation from Jesus until the end of the world. Thus he represents the third stage in the historico-salvational horizontal. The mountain represents nature or the first metaphysical vertical. The three disciples represent the incarnate spirits, that is, personal beings capable of ascending the mountain in order to receive God's Word or to transcend themselves in the direction of God in order to share with Him a friendly dialogue. Thus they represent the second stage in the metaphysical vertical. The transfigured Christ represents the third stage in the metaphysical vertical because He is the pinnacle of creation, the God-man, the only mediator between God and men, the center of the history of salvation and the glorified eschaton.

Byzantine liturgical tradition was very much aware of these views and painted this all-embracing panorama in the hymns sung during the Vespers of the Feast of the Transfiguration:[17]

O Lord, when You were transfigured on a high mountain in the presence of Your foremost disciples, You radiated with glory, showing how those who lead an outstanding life of virtue will be made worthy of the glory of heaven. Elias and Moses, conversing with the Lord, showed Him to be the Lord of the Living and the Dead, God who spoke through the Law and the Prophets—the same to whom the Father's voice bore witness out of the bright cloud, saying: "Hear Him, for it is He, through his Cross, who despoiled Hades and granted eternal life to the dead."

Transfiguration of Israel

In this context we have to remark that the giving of the Law by God through Moses to the Old Israel carried with it the idea and reality of Transfiguration. This is so because Yahweh entered into a covenant with Israel and Israel became His bride. Yahweh gave the Law to Israel in order to transfigure the Israelite community and each of its members. Thus He gave to Israel means of justification and preparation for their mission in the history of salvation. All the Israelites were thus obliged to transfigure their moral life according to the Decalogue and the code of love contained in Deuteronomy 6,5: "Thou shalt love the Lord thy God with thy whole heart and with thy whole soul and with thy whole strength." The inner life of the Israelite community was transfigured by the law of love contained in Leviticus 19,18: "Seek not revenge, nor be mindful of the injury of the citizen. Thou shalt love thy friend as thyself. I am the Lord."

These were the cornerstones of the transfiguration of Israel, which was a chosen people and out of which had to come the Transfigurer, the Son of Man and the Son of God, as well as the ·transfigured Lord, who stood along with Moses and Elias before His bewildered and stupefied disciples on the New Mount Sinai. The divine appearance or theophany and the voice of God the Father emanating from the cloud 'This is my beloved Son; hear him' was actually a New Law pronounced by God the Father. It was He who spoke His eternal Word into the world in order to transfigure it according to His eternal design. And His Incarnate Word was the New Law and its contents. Thus the New People of God were obliged to receive the God-man Jesus Christ as the New Law and were obliged to transfigure their lives according to Him, i.e. in mystical union with Him and for Him as their ultimate goal.

The awareness of the parallel between Mount Sinai and Mount Thabor, as well as between the Old and the New Dispensation, which is eschatological in nature, is expressed by this Byzantine liturgical text (Vespers of the Transfiguration, at the Apostichon):[18]

> He who mysteriously spoke to Moses on Mount Sinai and said: "I am who I am," today manifests Himself to His disciples on Mount Thabor and reveals through His Person that human nature is re-established in its original splendor. As witnesses to this grace and partakers of this joy, He raised up Moses and Elias, the forerunners of the glorious and saving Resurrection made possible by the Cross of Christ.

In this text Christ is portrayed as "ho ōn," i.e. "the existent," or "He who is" (the inscription in the halo of the Savior on most Byzantine icons). Thus our existence is a participation in His existence; our immortality—a participation in His immortality; our life derives from His divine life; our resurrection is made possible by His Resurrection.

Also in the Transfiguration Jesus revealed for a short moment to His three disciples the eschatological glory of the transfigured cosmos, the Church, and each of the blessed in heaven. He Himself was the first to undergo this mysterious eschatological transfiguration on Mount Thabor and on the Easter Sunday of His glorious Resurrection, because He is "the firstborn of every creature" (Col. 1,15) and "the firstborn from the dead, that in all things he may have the first place" (Col. 1,18). Thus the transfigured and resurrected Lord is the archetype of the transfigured and glorified extra-divine reality at the end of time:[19]

> O Lord, as a preparation to Your crucifixion, You led some of Your disciples to a high mountain and became transfigured before them, enlightening them with a radiation of light and glory. In this way, You showed the reality of the resurrection You are to grant us, in Your love for men and Your almighty power as God. Make us worthy of this resurrection, O God, for You are gracious and the Lover of Mankind.

Earth and Heaven

This brings us to a very serious eschatological question, concerning the continuity or discontinuity of the present world with "a new heaven and a new earth" (Isa. 65,17; 66,22; 2 Pet. 3,13 and Apoc. 21,1) at the end of time. We know that in the time pre-destined by God the present world or the world which will reach the end of a natural evolution or perhaps by some sort of entropic condition, will be delivered by God to destruction or assigned by Him to a mysterious transfiguration. One thing remains certain: the cosmos will not exist forever in its present evolving state. On one hand we may not ignore numerous texts pointing to the cata-strophic end of the world (e.g. Mt. ch. 24,1—ch. 25, v. 46; 2 Pet. 3,10-13). On the other hand there are texts which point to a trans-formation or transfiguration of the world by the power of the omnipotent God, e.g. Apoc. 21,1-8.

First of all the account of a renovation of all things at the end of time has a very striking resemblance to the account of creation recorded in the book of Genesis. Therefore one theological fact is certain: just as God the Alpha or the Creator experienced no dif-ficulty in the act of creation, likewise the same God acting as Omega or the Consummator will experience no difficulty in the act of the final fulfillment of the world. It is indeed one and the same divine and transfiguring "dynamis" at work in both cases or God in His transcendent and immanent dynamism.

Secondly we must reject the idea of an annihilation of the present world by an omnipotent act of God and the creation of a new one, because this contradicts the witness of the Bible and di-vine wisdom. Besides there are many biblical texts which eluci-date the mystery still further, e.g. in Mt. 19,28 are recorded the following words of Jesus directed to His disciples: "Amen I say to you that you who have followed me, in the *regeneration* when the Son of Man shall sit on the throne of his glory, shall also sit on twelve thrones, judging the twelve tribes of Israel."

The crucial words "in the regeneration" read in the Greek text "en ti palingenesis" which is translated by all good scholars as "new birth, re-birth, renovation."

The idea of transformation or transfiguration of the cosmos is expressed by St. Paul in Rom. 8,18-21. In this text we can dis-tinguish two distinct moments: the liberation of creation from the curse which rests on it and the glorification of it by its sharing in "the glory of the sons of God."

In ultimate analysis the text in Rom. 8,18-21 does not exclude the possibility of a supernatural transformation or transfiguration of the cosmos by the infinite and omnipotent power of God with all its visible and invisible manifestations, which are pictorially presented as fire, heat, great violence and dissolution of the old forms.

But it would be a mistake to restrict the mystery of the Transfiguration of the cosmos to the future only. Therefore, we have to distinguish between the eschatological and definitive transfiguration which will take place in the unknown and distant future and the eschatological but constantly progressing and contemporary transfiguration of man and the cosmos.

Here a quotation from *Katholische Dogmatik* by Michael Schmaus is in order:[20]

> The Resurrection is the beginning of the Transfiguration of the World. It exercises a function of fulfillment both for human history and for the whole of creation. History and the universe cohere to such an extent, that what happens in one dimension, affects also the other. History is not taking place outside extrahuman creation, but in it and through it. And vice versa the universe also has its meaning in human history. (Thus, as a result of the ontological nexus between the cosmos and man, it is reasonable that man attempt to appropriate the cosmos). The Transfiguration of creation which was commenced in the Resurrection and Transfiguration of Jesus Christ is exercising its dynamic influence upon men and through them upon the cosmos.

Again the Byzantine Liturgy is of great help to a theologian who tries to decipher the meaning of this realized eschatology in its cosmological and anthropological dimensions:[21]

> *Stichon:* Yours is the heaven and Yours the earth: You have founded the earth and made all it contains.

> 2. When David, the forefather of the Lord, foresaw in spirit Your coming in the flesh, he invited the whole creation to rejoice, crying out prophetically: "O Savior, Thabor and Hermon shall rejoice in Your name," for indeed You ascended this mountain with Your disciples. Through Your Transfiguration, You returned Adam's nature to its original splendor, re-

storing its very elements to the glory and brilliance of Your divinity. Wherefore we cry out to You, the Creator of all: "Glory to You!"

Transforming of the Eschaton

The glorious Transfiguration of the Lord does not only prefigure His Resurrection but also the cosmic transformation at the time of the eschatological *parousia* or the second and glorious coming of the Lord, which is alluded to in this liturgical text:[22]

> O Christ God, when You willed to prefigure Your Resurrection, You chose three disciples, Peter, James and John, and went up with them to Mount Thabor. At the moment of Your Transfiguration, O Savior, the mountain was flooded with light and Your disciples fell with their faces to the ground, for they could not bear the sight of Your countenance upon which no one may look, O Word! Angels attended with trembling and awe, the heavens were afraid and the earth shook to its very foundations when they saw the Lord of Glory come upon the earth.

Similar theological vision can be detected in the Armenian Liturgy:[23]

"This day Mount Thabor has flourished and is filled with luminous flowers. For Jesus blossomed in the body and manifested the glory of Adam."

In this context we have to recognize the greatness of science and the important function of scientists. We can safely say that all the discoveries of the natural sciences, all the inventions and applications of them, make new progress on our way of discovery of the new aspects of God. Thus the natural sciences help not only to discover the glory of God invested in the world, but also actively participate in the transfiguration of the world.

The same, but to a higher degree of intensity, can be said of the fine arts, which by word, sound, movement, paint and form make mute nature speak and force it to reveal its enigma. All the fine arts to a much higher degree of intensity than the natural sciences reveal to us the creativity of the incarnate spirit and in consequence some new aspects of God. Each real art by its creative intuition and spiritual penetration of inanimate nature exercises its primary duty of glorification of God by its very existence. But also their function of transfiguration of the world may not be overlooked. And this is why the poets and other artists are described as "inspired" or "full of God" or "full of divine inspiration" even in the extra-Christian realm. They are distinguished representatives of a transfigured mankind as well as transfigurers.

The scientists by inductive and deductive, empirical method, measure created reality and discover the external relationships of its different parts. All artists on the other hand by their creative intuition are unfolding to us the inner aspect or essences of things. But all of them as mentioned above are the transfigurers and the transfigured. By extension we can say that each new thought, impression, knowledge, wish of the will, emotion, feeling, etc. of an incarnate spirit or the psycho-somatic unity of man is part of the mystery of the Transfiguration of man and cosmos.

Transcendence and Immanence

One could object that this is an exaggerated view stained by mysticism and not consonant with modern theological trends. However, such an objection can grow up only in the context of a minimalist theology concerned primarily with the transcendence of God and overlooking His infinite immanence.[24] If we take the divine immanence and omnipotence seriously and harmonize it with the divine transcendence, then no serious difficulty can possibly present itself to us. I attempted to elucidate the coexistence of the divine transcendence with the divine immanence in the past:[25]

> By denying formally and materially all sorts of pantheism and by affirming the infinite immanence of God in the created extra-divine reality, we are affirming divine transcendence or at least we are pointing out one of its aspects because it is true to say that God is so perfectly and infinitely transcendent, that even His infinite immanence does not diminish it, but on the contrary heightens it.
>
> It was said a long time ago that God is more present to creatures than creatures can be present to themselves. It is equally true, that the heightening of the creature's presence to God, and by the same token the heightening of God's immanence to the creature, does not destroy the individuality, liberty, being, personality, or any other property of the creature. On the contrary, it heightens them, because the heightening of the closeness to God is an expression on the part of the creature of its transcen-

dence, or self-transcendence: it comes closer to itself in coming closer to the ground of all being, God Himself.

God is transcendent, not only because He stands infinitely above, apart and outside created, finite, and relative extra-divine reality, but also because He can by His infinite immanence penetrate, put-Himself-in-the-presence-of, sustain, govern, this extra-divine reality to such an infinite extent, that on the one hand He does not destroy created beings, and on the other hand "immanates" them so infinitely that He reaches into the core of their existent being to spheres where they are no more and where He alone, the infinite God, can extend His infinite transcendence. Humanly and figuratively speaking, God is infinitely transcendent not only towards the "above," but also towards the "below": "within" and "through" creatures. In other words God is infinitely transcendent not only in what is customarily described as His immanence. Therefore we can call God the para-immanent, trans-immanent, or hyper-immanent ground of being. As a consequence, any attempt at minimizing His immanence is at the same time an attempt to minimize His transcendence.

It is relatively easy to apply this teaching to the mystery of Transfiguration. The para-immanent, trans-immanent, or hyper-immanent God as the ground of the being and activity of His creatures is a dynamic, omnipotent and all-embracing reality.

In His transcendent and immanent dynamism He leads His creatures to their final goal—the inner, supernatural and divine life and love of the Most Holy Trinity. But this leading, governing, and attracting of the creatures by God includes the mystery of Transfiguration or the transfiguratory activity of God.

On the other hand a correct definition of a creature must include the idea of transfigurability and transfiguration, because the transcendence or self-transcendence of any personal or irrational creature expresses itself by its coming closer to the ground of all being and activity, God the Transfigurer, by way of its transfiguration and in the case of a rational creature also by way of self-transfiguration.

The Cosmic Christ

Besides this metaphysical foundation, the mystery of transfiguration has also another one, namely, the Christological foundation. The Cosmic Christ, Christos Pantocrator (i.e. Christ the All-Ruler),[26] or the resurrected and transfigured Lord is the Transfigurer. In order to appreciate this statement we have to outline the teaching of Christos Pantocrator. First of all this teaching is rooted in the explicit witness of the Sacred Scriptures, e.g. in the Epistle to the Colossians 1,15-20 St. Paul teaches of Christ:

> He is the image of the invisible God, the firstborn of every creature. For in Him were created all things in the heavens and on the earth, things visible and things invisible, whether Thrones, or Dominations, or Principalities, or Powers. All things have been created through and unto Him, and He is before all creatures and in Him all things hold together. Again, He is the head of His body, the Church; He, who is the beginning, the firstborn from the dead, that in all things He may have the first place. For it has pleased God the Father that in Him all His fullness should dwell and that through Him He should reconcile to Himself all things, whether on the earth or in the heavens, making peace through the blood of His cross.

On this text of the Sacred Scriptures as on many similar ones (Jo. 1,1-18; 17,1-26; Mt. 28,16-20; Rom. 8,18-22; Eph. 1,3-23; Heb. 1,1-2; 2,1) is based the doctrine of Christ the All-Ruler or Pantocrator. But exactly who Christ is, the All-Ruler, was explained to us in relatively simple terms by Peter (Simon or Simeon) Ibn Hassân of Hadeth, the Maronite Patriarch of Antioch, in a letter to Pope Leo X, dated March 8, 1514:[27]

> . . . the Virgin conceived without seed the Son of God, and thus God became human man, He was God in human-flesh and in human soul dressed in human flesh: He was born, but He was not created; He Himself is the creator and born out of the omnipotent Father before all creatures, He created the glorious and intact Virgin Mary, who carried Him in (her) womb for nine months. He is God and true God, the only Son, the only Creator, true God, true light (He) whole (is) truth without suspicion, without doubt: He provides for the whole human race and He sees all creatures: in His hands are life and death, and after death He grants life. Nothing either in heaven, or on earth, or in the sea remains closed to Him. He is God and immaculate man: He is light and knowledge in the heavenly paradise: He is our good, our salvation, the way of our life, the gate of our life, the fountain of our perpetual life; and we believe and hold with a firm faith, that He is always our God Jesus Christ.

Practically the same doctrine, but in technical theological language is presented to us by Karl Adam:[28]

> As man, Christ is one with mankind; indeed with the entire created world, at whose head He stands. As God, He stands in a union of substance with

His Father, from whom He comes, and with the Holy Spirit, in which He encounters the Father. Standing in the world, one with the world, He towers up into the very heart of the Godhead, He is God Himself, one with the Father and the Holy Spirit. And so in His person, He draws the world up into the very neighborhood of the eternal Father, while on the other hand He emanates over the entire world the union He has with His Father. He binds God and His creation into such a close reciprocal relationship that He cancels and overcomes not only every abyss between God and His creation but also the infinite disparity that separates them by their very natures; Christ conquers not only religious and ethical remoteness but also ontological distance. The God-man cancels out both the infinite remoteness of mere created being and the infinite remoteness of sinful being. So Christ is the substantial bond which brings together the most disparate antinomies. The Lord's sublime prayer that mankind "may be one even as we are one: I in them and thou in me; that they may be perfected in unity" is perfectly fulfilled in the God-man (cf. Scheeben, *Mysterien des Christentums*, pp. 350f.).

Into God's Unity

Thus the decisive Christological foundation of a continuous transfiguration consists in the double motion which constitutes the mediation and the pantocratic function of Christ, i.e. an upward motion or a constant drawing up of the entire extra-divine reality into the unity with God the Father and a downward motion or a constant emanation over the entire extra-divine reality of the unity He has with His Father. This dynamic two-way motion is based on the dynamics of the divine love: it is creative, and as a consequence transfiguratory in its effects.

Since Christ the All-Ruler is also the Transfigurer *par excellence* the Christians of the first centuries and the substantial majority of the Christians of Eastern Rites today feel that they already here on earth live in the Kingdom of God, which as yet is definitively inchoative, i.e. not perfect or fulfilled or definitively transfigured by Him. As a result of this conviction and religious experience, Oriental Christians feel that they must transfigure the world according to the image of Christ, who in turn is the perfect image of God the Father.

Evidently the first domain which must be shaped or transfigured according to Christ is the place of worship or the Church. Therefore, the Church is shaped like a cross and covered with a dome which symbolizes the supernaturally transfigured cosmos. Inside the Church the frescoes and the holy icons proclaim to all the constantly present mysteries of the Christian Faith. Especially the iconostasis (the screen-wall covered with icons which separates the altar from the place of the people) is a symbol and inchoative reality of the future beatific vision, which unfolds to us the future transfigured Kingdom of God with all its mysteries, the history of salvation which leads to it and especially Christ the lover of Man.

In the second row of icons on the iconostasis, among the principal liturgical feast-days the icon of the Transfiguration of our Lord is found. This icon is always the first one to be painted by a newly consecrated icon-painter in the Byzantine Rite churches. The vestments of the celebrants represent the vestments of the Transfigured Lord and so on. Thus the Christians of the Eastern Churches are very much aware of the mystery of Transfiguration in their liturgical and generally religious experience. They live in an eager expectation of the *Parousia* or the second and glorious coming of the Lord, which will replace the symbolic, mystic, and Eucharistic presence of the Lord by a glorious, transfigured and visible reality.

It will be the same Son of Man who was depicted by the prophet Daniel (7,13-14) and who refused the "semeion" or the messianic "sign" the Jews were asking for and promised them only the "sign of Jonah," that is, death and Resurrection. It will be, however, the same Son of Man who gave the very "sign" to the three chosen disciples on Mount Thabor. It will be the same transfigured Son of Man, who appeared in His glory to the seer of the Apocalypse as the transfigurer and consummator of the history of salvation and of the cosmos (Apoc. 1,12-13).

In this context we have to correct one view, which points to wrong theological accentuation in the analysis of the mystery of the Transfiguration of our Lord. It is usually stressed very strongly that Christ wanted to prove to His disciples His divinity and thus to avert from them the future scandal of His passion.

This is quite clear from the Kontakion of the feast of "the

Holy Transfiguration of our Lord and God and Savior Jesus Christ" in the Byzantine Liturgy:[29]

> O Christ God, You were transfigured on the Mountain and Your disciples saw as much of Your glory as they could hold, so that seeing You crucified they would know You had willed to suffer Your passion and would proclaim to the world that You are verily the Reflection of the Father.

The Humanity of Christ

However, it seems that the accentuation must be placed on the revelation of the sacred humanity of Jesus as the instrument of His cosmic and redemptive Lordship which was the transfigurable and transfigured archetype of the Church, the whole of humanity, and the whole cosmos. Actually it is the very seat and source of the transfigurability and transfiguration.

Now we are ready to ask a very important theological and existential question: is the sacred humanity of Jesus at work here and now as the instrument of the transfiguration? The answer is a categorical "yes." This is so because the Church itself is a transfigured people of God. Moreover, she is the body of Christ. The Sacraments as the visible signs of the invisible graces are the meeting places and events which invite us to the living, suffering, resurrected and transfigured Lord. Thus they are the living mysteries and also means of the invisible transfiguration here and now and warrants of the future and definitive transfiguration at the end of time.

The same in a lesser degree of intensity, of course, can be said of the sacramentals which are imparted to persons or pronounced over the material reality surrounding us. By imparting them the Church is pronouncing them as the good creatures of God. She liberates them from the power of evil, but actually pronounces over them her prophetic benediction and indicates that the divine transfiguring power is at work in them and that they are the transfigurable existents that will reach the ultimate fulfillment at the end of time.

A close look at the theological significance of the miracles of Jesus and miracles in general reveals besides the cosmic lordship of Jesus also a dimension of the transfiguration of the visible and invisible reality. The forgiveness of sins which usually accompanied the miracles of healing wrought by Jesus were pointing to the mystery of man, who as a psycho-somatic whole was destined to participate in the mystery of transfiguration in the totality of His person, including all integral and metaphysical parts as well as all of His dimensions.

It becomes clear to us also that in the assumption of the Mother of God in body and soul to the glory of heaven we have to see a case of a total break-through of the *eschata*. This is so because the love and omnipotence of God through the instrumentality of the sacred humanity of Jesus wrought a total transfiguration of the whole person of the Blessed Mother of God at the end of her earthly course. The so-called coronation of the Blessed Virgin Mary as the Queen of heaven is nothing else than an anthropomorphic presentation of the same mystery, because her dormition, assumption and glorification in heaven are three aspects of the same mystery of her transfiguration by the Triadic God. As the archetype and mother of the Church she was undergoing in her being the transfiguration which will be given from above to the whole Church and the cosmos.

In this context the reformation or renewal of the Church must be seen primarily as a transfiguration coming from above and only secondarily as the work of man coming from below. Also the expression "reformata semper reformanda" can have its proper meaning only in a context of a continuous transfiguration coming from God as His loving gift. Therefore a transfiguring renewal of the Church as part of the Kingdom of God must be a constant renewal of a lively communion with the community of the blessed or the Church in Heaven.

The personalist philosophy of our day could be of great help in the elucidation of eschatology as a personal and transfiguring encounter of man (understood both as a collective and individual reality) with the saving, sanctifying, transfiguring and fulfilling tri-personal reality of the Triadic God and those who were transfigured by Him and entered into His inner life and love.

Church Renewal

The renewal of the Church, therefore, is primarily an intensification of this transfiguring inner life and love of the Triadic God in us, that is in each of us individually and in the community of the Church. Therefore, all changes of liturgy, of discipline, the structure of the Church, etc. must be subordinated to the primary reality indicated above and its intensification in our lives. Therefore, any renewal of the Church in separation from the mystery of Transfiguration is like the construction of the Tower of Babel and is doomed to disintegration.

The last major aspect of the mystery of Transfiguration with which I would like to deal in this paper concerns the Holy Spirit.[30] It is the Holy Spirit or the Third Person of the Most Holy Trinity who gives us the prerequisites and fruits of a real Christian existence. With Christ Our Lord, who was the "pneumataphor" *par excellence*, or the principal carrier of the Spirit of God, the same Spirit is co-transfigurer of ourselves, of the Church and the cosmos. And thus He transfigures us by giving us knowledge and love (Eph. 1,17f; 3,14-21; 2 Thess. 3,5), peace and joy (Rom. 15,33; Gal. 5,22; 2 Thess. 3,16) and unity (Rom. 15,5). But His primary function is to be the Spirit of truth, who reminds us of Christ and His heavenly Father and prompts us to witness and prayer (Jo. 14,25-26; 15,26-27; 16,5-16). His gracious transfiguring activity comes to us as a call or a warning or a strengthening or a consolation or an illumination of our minds.

The same Spirit transfigures us by opening our hearts and by moving us to the realization of our sinful condition and by reverting us from it and converting us to Christ with a prayerful contrition (Acts 2,40; 9,31; 11,22f; 13,15; 14,14; Rom. 8,28-30; 12,8; I Cor. 14,3; II Cor. 8,4; Heb. 12,5; I Tim. 4,13). Thus it is the Spirit of God, who transfigures us and makes us capable to speak the faithful and prayerful "yes" to Jesus the Lord (I Cor. 12,13; I Jo. 4,2-3; I Cor. 2,12-15; Eph. 1,17-18). He gives to the human spirit an internal witness, that the human being is a child of God (Rom. 8,16; I Jo. 3,19-24). He also prays in the human being when it is silent before God (Rom. 8,26f; I Jo. 2,20-27; Jo. 16,13).

The consciousness of this biblical teaching concerning the Holy Spirit and His activity is very vivid in Oriental Christianity. We see this in one of the most solemn acts in the Byzantine Liturgy: the Epiclesis or invocation of the Holy Spirit which is recited silently by the priest after the consecration.

The second example of a transfiguring activity of the Holy Spirit is a short prayer, which I think has nothing comparable to it in the whole of Christianity. Besides being a very beautiful prayer, it is also an exposition of dogmatic theology concerning the Divine Person of the Spirit. Also, a special mention should be made of the omnipotence of the same Spirit and His all-embracing and transfiguratory activity, which is not restricted to human souls only, but extends to all things of the visible and the invisible cosmos. It reads:

> O Heavenly King, Comforter, Spirit of Truth, who art everywhere and fulfillest all things, Treasury of good and giver of life, come and dwell in us, and cleanse us from every stain, and save our souls, O good One.

Theosis

In conclusion, let me highlight the fact that the essence of Christianity consists in an active participation in the inner life and love of the Triadic God. Technically this participation is called *theosis*[31] in Greek, that is, the mystery of divine grace or divinization (not deification!) of man and of the transfigured in Christ cosmos. *Theosis* as the mystery of union with and the assimilation to the Triadic God in its eschatological dimension gives the last meaning to all the other mysteries of Christianity, i.e. Creation, Incarnation, Redemption, the Church, Ascension of Our Lord, Assumption of the Mother of God and of the Transfiguration. This is so because *theosis* is mysteriously and intimately connected with the inner and outer glory of the Triadic God. However, there is no *theosis* without the Transfiguration, because the last is a process leading to *theosis* or divinization as well as its integral part. Without *theosis* and transfiguration there can be no salvation. Without them there is also no real mystical spirituality, which tries to penetrate through concrete and visible reality into the realm of the invisible, eternal and divine, stressing not the statistical and material quantities of the Christian existence, but the spiritual qualities and their supernatural dynamism.

Let us conclude with a Troparion of the feast of the Holy Transfiguration in the Byzantine Liturgy:[32]

> O Christ our God, at the time of Your Transfiguration on the Mount, You showed Your disciples as much of Your glory as they could hold. Through the prayers of the Mother of God, let Your eternal light shine also upon us sinners. O Giver of Light, glory to You!

Postscript

A theological meditation by its very nature is neither systematic nor exhaustive. However, it helps to analyse some of the known aspects of the subject in question and unveils some new ones. Thus it is related to contemplation for it is performed in faith and takes into account truth, beauty and goodness of the object under consideration. Many aspects were quite consciously left out of the present meditation, e.g. the "negative" transfiguration (sin, damnation, "second death"); patristic and mediaeval witnesses; Eastern and Western liturgical traditions etc. Therefore this theological meditation was meant as an invitation to further study and scholarly research in this relatively unexplored area.

FOOTNOTES

1. Select bibliography on Transfiguration in the Bible: F. J. Badcock, "The Transfiguration": *Journal of Theological Studies* 22 (1921) 321-326; M. Balagué, "La Transfiguración": *Cultura Biblica* 24/217 (1967) 356-365; Idem, "La Transfiguración": *Revista Biblica* 29/129 (1967) 51-58; H. Baltensweiler, *Die Verklärung Jesu. Historisches Ereignis und synoptische Berichte* (Zürich 1959); J. Blinzler, *Die neutestamentlichen Berichte uber die Verklärung Jesu* (Münster 1937); J. Blinzler—E. Sauser, "Verklärung Jesu": *Lexikon fur Theologie und Kirche* (1965²) 10:709-712; G. H. Boobyer, "St. Mark and the Transfiguration": *Journal of Theological Studies* 41 (1940) 119-140; Idem, *St. Mark and the Transfiguration Story* (Edinburgh 1942); P. Dabek, "Siehe es erschien Moses und Elias (Mt. XVIII,-

3)": *Biblica* (1942) 175-189; G. B. Caird, "The Transfiguration": *The Expository Times* 67 (1955-56) 291-294; C. E. Carlston, "Transfiguration and Resurrection": *Journal of Biblical Literature* 80 (1961) 233-240; M. Coune, "Baptême, Transfiguration et Passion": *Nouvelle Revue Theologique* 102/2 (1970) 165-179; E. Dabrowski, *La Transfiguration de Jesus* (Rome 1939); A.-M. Denis, "Une theólogie de la Redemption. La Transfiguration chez S. Marc": *La Vie Spirituelle* 41 (1959) 136-149; F. X. Durwell, "La transfiguration de Jésus": *La Vie Spirituelle* 35 (1951) 115-126; Dom Egender, "La Transfiguration": *Terre Sainte* 7-8 (1969) 162-167; A. Feuillet, "Les perspectives propres à chaque évangeliste dans les récits de la Transfiguration": *Biblica* 39 (1958) 281-301; A. George, "La Transfiguration": *Bible et Vie Chretien* 33 (Mar. 1960) 21-25; G. H. Guyot, "Transfiguration": *New Catholic Encyclopedia* (New York, etc. 1967) 14:243-244; S. Lewis Johnson, Jr., "The Transfiguration of Christ": *Bibliotheca Sacra* 124/494 (1967) 133-143; A. Kenny, "The Transfiguration and the Agony in the Garden": *The Catholic Biblical Quarterly* 19 (1957) 444-452; H. P. Müller, "Die Verklärung Jesu. Eine motivgeschichtliche Studie": *Zeitschrift fur die neutestamentliche Wissenschaft und die Kunde der alteren Kirche* 51 (1960) 56-64; H. Riesenfeld, *Jesus transfigure. L'arriereplan du recit evangelique de la transfiguration de Notre-Seigneur* (Lund 1947); L. F. Rivera, "Interpretatio Transfigurationis Jesu in redactione evangelii Marci": *Verbum Domini* 46 (1968) 99-104; M. Sabbe, "De Transfiguratië van Jesus": *Collationes Brugenses et Gandavenses* 4 (1958) 467-503; Idem, "La rédaction du récit de la Transfiguration": *La venue du Messie*, E. Massaux, ed. (=*Recherches Bibliques* IV; Louvain 1962) 65-100; G. Schneider, "Verklärung": *Bibel-Lexikon*, H. Haag, edit. (Einsiedeln /1951 ff/ 1968) 1826f; F. C. Synge—D. Baly, "The Transfiguration Story": *The Expository Times* 82/3 (1970) 82-83; J.-M. Vosté, *De Baptismo, Tentatione et Transfiguratione Jesu* (Romae 1934) 115-167 (=Vol. 2, *Studia Theologiae Biblicae Novi Testamenti*, Romae 1933-37; 3 vol.); D. A. Wilmart, "Transfigurare": *Bulletin d'ancienne litterature et d'archeologie chretiennes* 1 (1911) 282-292; B. Zielinski, "De Doxa transfigurati": *Verbum Domini* 26 (1948) 291-303; Idem, "De Transfigurationis sensu": *Verbum Domini* 26 (1948) 335-343; J. A. Ziesler, "The Transfiguration Story and the Markan Soteriology": *The Expository Times* 81/9 (1970) 263-268.

2. Select bibliography on Transfiguration in Art: F. M. Abel, "Notes d' archéologie chrétienne sur le Sinaï: la mosaïque de l'abside": *Revue Biblique* (1907) 105-108; V. Benesevic, "Sur la date de la mosaïque de la Transfiguration au Mont Sinaï": *Byzantion* 1 (1924) 145-172; Ch. Diehl, *Iustinien et la civilisation byzantine au VIe siecle* (Paris 1901) fig. 107, p. 295; E. Dinkler, *Das Apsismosaik von S. Apollinare in Classe* (Köln-

Oplade 1964); Ch. Ihm, *Die Programme der christlichen Apsismalerei vom 4. Jh. bis zur Mitte des 8. Jh.* (Wiesbaden 1960) 69-75; K. Künstle, *Ikonographie der christlichen Kunst,* vol. 1, *Prinzipienlehre—Hilfsmotive —Offenbarungstatsachen* (Freiburg i. Br. 1928) 403-408; G. Mesini, "La Trasfigurazione a S. Apollinare nel mosaico della Basilica Classense": *Illustrazione Vaticana* 5 (1934) 661-664; G. Millet, *Recherches sur l'iconographie de l'Evangile aux XIVe, XVe et XVIe s.dans les monuments de Mistra, de la Macedoine et du Mt Athos* (Paris 1916) 216-231; A Pigler, *Barockthemen* (Budapest 1956) I, 290-295; S. Vailhé, "La mosaique de la Transfiguration au Sinaï est-elle de Justinien?": *Revue de l'Orient Chretien,* 2e Sêrie, 2 (1907) 96-98; A. de Waal, "Zur Ikonographie der Transfiguratio in der altchristlichen Kunst": *Romische Quartalschrift* 16 (1902) 25-40; Idem, *Die Verklärung auf Tabor in Liturgie und Kunst* (München 1913); O. Wulff, *Altchristliche und byzantinische Kunst* (Berlin 1922) II, 419, fig. 364.

3. There are notable exceptions to the general rule which contain theological aspects of the mystery of transfiguration, e.g.: J. L. Cypriano, "Transfiguration (Theological Aspect)": *New Catholic Encyclopedia* (New York etc. 1967) 14:224-225; F. X. Durwell, *In the Redeeming Christ,* tr. R. Sheed (New York 1963); M. Eichinger, *Die Verklärung Christi bei Origenes. Die Bedeutung des Menschen Jesu in seiner Christologie* (Wien 1969 = *Wiener Beitrage zur Theologie XXIII*); J. Höller, *Die Verklärung Jesu* (Freiburg i. Br. 1937); A. Loisy, "La Transfiguration": *Revue d'Histoire et Litterature Religieuse* (1907) 464-482; J. R. Macphail, *The Bright Cloud. The Bible in the Light of the Transfiguration* (London 1956); P. Miquel, "Le mystère de la transfiguration": *Questions liturgiques et paroissiales* 42 (1961) 194-223; A. Penna èt alii, "Trasfigurazione": *Enciclopedia Cattolica* (Città del Vaticano 1954) XII, 436-441; A. M. Ramsey, *The Glory of God and the Transfiguration of Christ* (London 1949); J. W. C. Wand, *Transfiguration* (London 1967).

4. Cf. L. K. Shook, editor, *Theology of Renewal. Proceedings of the Congress on the Theology of Renewal of the Church, Centenary of Canada 1867-1967* (Montreal 1968) 2 vol.

5. P. B. T. Bilaniuk, "Church Renewal Affects Individual": *The Canadian Register,* September 2, 1967, p. 15.

6. On the liturgical texts concerning the feast of Transfiguration of Our Lord cf. *Mynia, misjac avgust* (Kiev 1894). On the interpretation of the same feast cf. S. V. Bulgakov, *Nastolnaja Kniga dla svjashchenno-cerkovno-sluzytelej* (Charkov 1900) 271-275; K. Dienst, "Verklärungsfest": *Religion in Geschichte und Gegenwart*[3], VI,1358; J. B. Ferreres, "La Transfiguration de Notre Seigneur. Histoire de la Fête: *Ephemerides Theologicae Lovanienses* (1928) 630-643; J. Larisis, *Ho metamorfosis tou Soteros*

hemon Jesou Christou (Athinai 1960); J. Leclerq, "L'office de la Transfiguration composé par Pierre le Vénerable": *Pierre le Venerable* (1946) 379-390; K. Nikolskij, *Posobije k izucheniju Bogosluzenia Pravoslavnoj Cerkvi* (S.-Peterburg 1900) 569-570: A. de Waal, *Die Verklärung auf Tabor in Liturgie und Kunst* (München 1913).

7. The liturgical texts quoted in this paper are taken from *Byzantine Daily Worship*, J. Raya—J. de Vinck, editors and translators (Alleluia Press; Allendale, N.J. and Combermere, Ont. 1969) 744-751. Abbreviation used here: *BDW*.

8. *BDW* 747.

9. *BDW* 745.

10. *BDW* 746.

11. Cf. P. Teilhard de Chardin, *Le Phenomene humain* (Paris 1955). English translation by Bernard Wall, *The Phenomenon of Man* (New York 1959).

12. *Oeuvres de Pierre Teilhard de Chardin*, vol. 9, *Science et Christ* (Paris 1965) 213.

13. *Hymn of the Universe* (New York 1965) 133.

14. *Le Milieu Divin* (London 1960) 44.

15. *Hymn of the Universe*, transl. by Gerald Vann, O. P. (New York 1965) 41-55. Cf. also the translation by Noël Lindsay, "Christ in Matter": *Harper's Bazaar* (December 1962) pp. 70, 128-129.

16. *Katholische Dogmatik* (München 1962[6]) II,1,p. 136f.

17. *BDW* 746-747.

18. *BDW* 748.

19. *BDW* 746.

20. *Katholische Dogmatik* (München 1963[6]) II,2,p. 461.

21. *BDW* 748.

22. *BDW* 747.

23. *Divine Liturgy of the Armenian Apostolic Orthodox Church*, transl. by Tiran Nersoyan (The Delphic Press, New York 1950) 165.

24. On the immanence and transcendence of God cf. M. Schmaus, *Katholische Dogmatik* (München 1962[6]) II,1,p. 109; cf. also p. 41 (Bibl.).

25. Petro Bilaniuk, "The Christology of Teilhard de Chardin": *Proceedings of the Teilhard Conference 1964* (Fordham University, New York 1965) 115-116.

26. Cf. A. D. Galloway, *The Cosmic Christ* (London 1951); C. F. Mooney, *Teilhard de Chardin and the Mystery of Christ* (New York 1966); G. A. Maloney, S.J., *The Cosmic Christ from Paul to Teilhard* (New York 1968); R. Hale, *Christ and the Universe. Teilhard de Chardin and the Cosmos*, edited by M. Meilach (Chicago 1973).

27. Caesaris S.R.E. Card. Baronii, Od. Raynaldi et Jac. Laderchii, *Annales Ecclesiastici . . .*, Tomus XXXI (1513-1526) (Barri Ducis Parisiis 1877)

a.1514, n.89.

28. *The Christ of Faith. The Christology of the Church* (New York 1962) 238.
29. *BDW* 746.
30. On the teaching of the Holy Spirit in Eastern Christianity see: Serge Boul-gakof, *Le Paraclet* (Paris 1944); A. Schmemann, *The World as Sacrament* (New York 1966) 81-99; P. A. Florensky, "The Holy Spirit": *Ultimate Questions,* edit. by A. Schmemann (Holt, Rinehart and Winston 1965) 137-173; T. Hopko, "Holy Spirit in Orthodox Theology and Life": Holy Spirit. Commonweal Papers 3, *Commonweal,* Vol. LXXXIX, No. 6 (Nov. 8, 1968) 186-191; Paul Evdokimoff, *L'Esprit Saint dans la tradition ortho-doxe* (Paris 1970).
31. Cf. Petro B. T. Bilaniuk, "The Mystery of *Theosis* or Divinization": *The Heritage of the Early Church: Essays In Honor of The Very Reverend Georges Vasilievich Florovsky on the Occasion of His Eightieth Birthday.* Edited by David Neiman and Margaret Schatkin (*Orientalia Christiana Analecta 195;* Rome, Pontifical Oriental Institute, 1973) 337-59.
32. *BDW* 746.

the mystery of theosis or divinization

Originally published in *The Heritage of the Early Church. Essays in Honor of the Very Reverend Georges Vasilievich Florovsky...on the occasion of his Eightieth Birthday.* Edited by David Neiman and Margaret Schatkin (Rome: Pont.Institutum Studiorum Orientalium, 1973; *Orientalia Christiana Analecta 195*), pp.337–359. Reprinted here with permission.

THE MYSTERY OF *THEOSIS* OR DIVINIZATION

by

Petro B. T. Bilaniuk

Introduction

Whenever a Western Christian commences to compare Eastern Orthodoxy with Roman Catholicism he usually starts from a generally accepted premise that there are no real differences in doctrine between the two, except in five major points. They are usually described as the stumbling blocks to re-union of the two major parts of Christianity. With greater or lesser variations they are traditionally enumerated as follows : 1. The Roman Primacy and papal infallibility ; 2. The " Filioque " question ; 3. Eucharistic differences (esp. *Epiclesis*), 4. Recent Marian dogmas, or the Immaculate Conception and the Assumption of the Mother of God, and 5. Eschatological differences (especially retribution after death and purgatory).[1] However a closer examination of the above enumerated controversial points of doctrine reveals quite clearly that the real differences, or even antagonistic and divisive issues, are of historical, cultural, philosophical, linguistic and emotional origin and that therefore they are not theological issues strictly speaking. The dividing factors are much more subtle, much more profound and firmly rooted in the diverse mentality and different *Weltanschauung* of the two divided parts of Christianity.[2]

The hamartiocentric and thanatocentric mentality of Western Christianity, that is a mentality which is profoundly pessimistic and almost pathologically obsessed by its primary concentration

---

[1] This enumeration is adopted by many authors, e. g. Angel Santos Hernández, S. J., *Iglesias de Oriente. Puntos especificos de su teologia* (Sal Terrae, Santander 1959) 119-312 ; G. A. Maloney, Orthodox Churches, In : *New Catholic Encyclopedia* (New York, etc. 1967) 10 : 795-796.

[2] On this see : A. Szeptycky, *Deux mentalités*, in : *Irenikon* (1926) 232-235 and 261-266. English translation : " Eastern and Western Mentality," in : *Commonweal* XII (Oct. 8, 1930) 570-574 ; also in *The Eastern Churches Quarterly* IX/8 (Winter 1952) 392-401 ; Deno J. Geanakoplos, *Byzantine East and Latin West : Two Worlds of Christendom in the Middle Ages and Renaissance* (Harper Torchbooks, New York and Evanston 1966).

22

on the problem and the mystery of evil, sin and death,[3] is alien to the spiritual optimism of Eastern Christianity and especially to its Alexandrian tradition, the chief concern of which was eternal life, light and love of the Triadic God and His loving presence to His creatures. I am therefore convinced that any meaningful ecumenical or theological dialogue must start from the above mentioned premise, or otherwise it will remain superficial and in the long run will produce no fruitful results.

The central and characteristic part and the cornerstone of the Eastern Christian optimism is a very lively awareness of and an intense contemplation of the complex of ideas pertaining to the mystery of *theosis* (θείωσις) or divinization in its creational, Triadic, Christological, Pneumatological, anthropological, ecclesial, cosmological and eschatological dimensions. Here a preliminary description of *theosis* is in place. *Theosis* or divinization (or sometimes even deification) can be described as the omnipotent and sanctifying, divine and Triadic activity which, because of the indwelling of the Trinity and grace and because of the inborn and natural capacity of the creature for transfiguration, induces a process of assimilation to God the Father of the whole human person, of mankind and of the visible and invisible universe in its totality, through the mediation of the incarnate Logos, Christ the Pantocrator, and in the Holy Spirit.

From the above preliminary description we can distinguish several moments in *theosis*. In its creational dimension, *theosis* connotes that any creature by the very fact of its creation by God is dependent on God and is an image of God. Therefore this creature is ontologically good and meaningful. It is placed at the beginning of a divinizing process and is destined to tend from God the Alpha, or the Creator, through the loving, divinizing presence of God, to Him as the Omega, or the final goal and consummator of reality.

The Christological moment of *theosis* is rooted in the presence of the Logos in the act of creation, through Whom, in Whom, and for Whom it took place, and in the pantocratic function and dignity of Christ the Lord, who by His Incarnation, Life, Doctrine, Miracles, Transfiguration, Death, Resurrection and Ascension

---

[3] These mysteries and connected problems have enjoyed great popularity in Western Christian tradition. Innumerable works based on different philosophical presuppositions have been written on these subjects. In many instances certain mystifications of evil tended to obscure the optimistic salvific message of the Gospel.

founded a new, divinized and divinizing reality or regenerated mankind called the Church. This new mysterious and eschatological community as the new mankind is in a simultaneous process of humanization and divinization [4] which is firmly rooted in the Christ-event which is its somatic foundation.

The pneumatic moment of *theosis*, and by the same token of the Church, is the Holy Spirit. With Christ the Cosmic Pantocrator, who is the pneumatophor *par excellence*, or the principal carrier and dispenser of the Spirit of God, the same Spirit is co-transfigurer and co-divinizer of man, the Church, and the Cosmos.[5]

Thus *theosis* according to the understanding of the Eastern Christians consists in an active participation in the inner life, light, and love of the Triadic God, which increases in intensity as the process of assimilation of the creature to God becomes faster and deeper. In the final eschatological fulfillment of the whole extradivine reality, theosis reaches its high point, but it is with the created reality from the first moment of its existence, at least in the lowest degree of its intensity.

This article is intended to supply the reader with a *status quaestionis* and a basic bibliography on *theosis*. The vast material dealing with this subject could not, of course, be handled within the scope of this article.

---

[4] The question of the relationship between the sacred and the profane, secular and holy, humanization and divinization, etc., assumes one of the first places in contemporary theological discussion. Probably the best contribution to this discussion can be found in the writings of P. Teilhard de Chardin, especially in *Le Milieu Divin* (Collins, London 1960) and " The Heart of the Problem ", in : *The Future of Man* (Harper and Row, New York 1964) 260-69.

[5] On Eastern Christian Pneumatology see : Serge Boulgakof, *Le Paraclet*, traduit du russe par Constantine Andronikof (Aubier, Paris 1944) ; P. A. Florensky, " The Holy Spirit ", in : *Ultimate Questions*, ed. A. Schmemann (Holt, Rinehart and Winston, New York 1965) 137-173 ; Thomas Hopko, " Holy Spirit in Orthodox Theology and Life ", *Commonweal* LXXXIX, No. 6 (Nov. 8, 1968) 186-192 ; Paul Evdokimoff, *L'Esprit Saint dans la tradition orthodoxe* (Paris, Editions du Cerf 1970.) Eastern Christian teaching on the Holy Pneuma is summarized in a short but beautiful prayer of the Byzantine Liturgy : " O Heavenly King, Comforter, Spirit of Truth, Who art everywhere and fulfillest all things, Treasury of good and Giver of life, come and dwell in us, and cleanse us from every stain, and save our souls, O Good One."

Theosis in the religions of the world [6]

Eastern Christian doctrine of *theosis* is not an isolated phenomenon in the world religions, because even a cursory evaluation of them reveals that in almost all of them there can be found some elements or at least traces of divinization or deification. In many of them this is portrayed as an eschatological life with God and in others it assumes pantheistic or monistic forms.

The whole effort of the Vedic philosophy and mysticism aims at achieving direct union with God. More exactly, the individual soul (atman) strives to achieve union with the world soul (brahma) through prayer, meditation, mortification, and inner purification.[7]

The Upanishads teach the salvation or the emancipation of the human spirit or soul from Mara, or the illusions, and its reunion or even merger with the infinite Brahma. Buddhist " nirvana ", interpreted as a dying out in the heart of passion, hatred, and delusion which induces a beatific spiritual condition and freedom from the necessity of future metempsychosis or transmigration of the soul, is a rather late phenomenon. Original Buddhist teaching seems to have been the one expressed by Buddha in the legend entitled *The Marriage-Feast in Jambunada* : " Let no man be single, let every one be wedded in holy love to the truth. And when Mara, the destroyer, comes to separate the visible forms of your being, you will continue to live in the truth, and you will partake of the life everlasting, for the truth is immortal." [8]

Nanak, the founder of Sikhism, taught that the only bliss in the beyond is the individuality-extinguishing-absorption of the faithful in the " True Name " (God). Sikhism, therefore, represents an extreme form of monistic eschatology.[9]

In ancient Egypt, especially in the time of Amarna, the deification of the living pharaoh was the official political ideology and religious belief. Such phenomena as drowning in the sacred river

---

[6] For a brief general survey see : E. Pax, *Vergöttlichung*, in : *Lexikon für Theologie und Kirche*[2] (Herder, Freiburg i. Br. 1965) 10 : 704-706. Many relevant texts can be found in : *The Great Asian Religions, An Anthology*, compiled by Wing-tsit Chan, et alii (Macmillan, London 1969). F. Heiler, *Erscheinungsformen der Religion* (Stuttgart 1961) 526 f. Eduard des Places, et alii, " Divinisation," in : *Dictionnaire de Spiritualité* (Paris 1957) III, 1370-1459.

[7] Cf. especially the following Hymns from the Rigveda : To Visvakarman (Book X, 81) ; Hymn to Man (Book X, 90) ; To Faith (Book X, 151).

[8] Lin Yutang, *The Wisdom of India* (Carlton House, New York 1942) 370.

[9] J. B. Noss, *Man's Religions* (Macmilian, London 1969[4]) 238.

Nile was interpreted as a road to deification. Also it was believed that in the imitation of the funeral rites of Osiris the dead person was re-uniting with God.[10]

Besides many different and quite often artificial rites and beliefs concerning the deification of the Emperor, king, or ruling monarch, antiquity exhibited many different mystery cults. The person initiated into these secret mysteries had to undergo many different rites, prayers, fasting, indoctrination, and finally an alleged liberation from the corporeal reality until he or she was ready for *epopteia*, or the divine vision through which he or she was thought to partake in the divine powers and the *soteria*, or salvation.[11] In the Hellenic world we find many different ideas of deification in the poets, in Orphism, Stoicism, Platonism, and the hermetic gnosis.[12]

In the teaching of Plato we find the philosophical concept of the imitation of and assimilation to God, which is presented as the most important task in man's moral and intellectual life. To this Plotinus added another feature, namely liberation from the body and union with God which is conceived as a beatitude. To this philosophical and theoretical teaching there corresponded in practice the deification of heroes of the Greek popular imagination.[13]

Gnosticism taught that there is a divine spark in man, which descends from the *Pleroma* (i. e. God Himself) into the evil world of matter. The problem of human existence is redemption, salvation, or liberation by assimilation of esoteric knowledge and illumination of the intellect, which makes it possible for the gnostic to ascend again to the good God and reach a mystical union with Him.[14]

Thus a tendency to divinization or even deification can be observed in many religions of the world. Therefore it seems that a natural tendency of man towards transcendence or self-transcend-

---

[10] Cf. S. Morenz, *Ägyptische Religion* (Stuttgart 1960).

[11] K. Prümm, *Religionsgeschichtliches Handbuch für den Raum der alt-christlichen Umwelt. Hellenistisch-römische Geistesströmungen und Kulte mit Beachtung des Eigenlebens der Provinzen* (Freiburg i. Br. 1943 ; Rom 1954).

[12] Eduard des Places, " Divinisation (I. Pensée religieuse des Grecs) ", in : *Dictionnaire de Spiritualité* (Paris 1957) III, 1370-75.

[13] On this see : O. Faller, *Griechische Vergottung und christliche Vergött-lichung*, in : *Gregorianum* 6 (1925) 405-435 ; P. Langlois, " Greek Philosophy (Religious Aspects)," in : *New Catholic Encyclopedia* (New York, etc. 1967) 6 : 736-742 ; M. P. Nilsson, *Griechische Religion* (München 1955) II, 661 ff. ; J. Gross, *La divinisation du chrétien d'après les pères Grecs* (Paris 1938) 1-69.

[14] G. W. MacRae, " Gnosticism," in : NCE 6 : 523-528.

ence towards the absolute, the infinite and the eternal, which is manifested in the religious phenomena of meditation, prayer, cult, moral responsibility, etc., must be interpreted primarily as a tendency towards divinization, or better as a process of divinization tending towards eschatological divinized fulfillment in a certain form of union with the Godhead. This leads me to conclude that *theosis* or divinization is an essential anthropological element which belongs necessarily to a real individual and collective human existence and which by itself contradicts many elements of contemporary secularization. This truth has been partly observed by Tertullian who spoke of the *testimonium animae naturaliter christianae* (Apol. 17,6 : P. L. 1,377).[15]

A philosophical interpretation of the active and passive divinization as observed in many religions can be summed up as follows : man, understood as an individual person or as a community of persons, is naturally capable of at least a limited knowledge of God and of the natural moral law. To his very essence and existence belongs also a life of cult, prayer, meditation and a tendency towards the mysterious, holy, numinous and occult, even if these elements at times exhibit false and atheistic traits.

To this a theological interpretation would add that man and the cosmos, as creatures of the Trinity redeemed by Christ the Pantocrator, and sanctified by the Spirit, are carriers of Trinitarian and Christological seals, and that they are also pneumatophores or carriers of the Spirit. Thus the obediential potency of man and the cosmos, or of the whole extra-divine reality, is actualized by an impulse of the divinizing grace in at least the lowest degree of intensity and initiates the process of divinization which progresses until the final fulfillment in the mysterious God the Omega.

The biblical foundation of theosis [16]

In the Old Testament the mystery of man was expressed in the doctrine of man as the image of God (Gen 1,27 ff). This pictorial similarity of man to God consists according to the Greek Church Fathers [17] in the reason, freedom and love of man, that is in qualities and gifts which man received from God in order to be God's friend and similar to Him. This however in no way de-

---

[15] Cf. P. B. Bilaniuk, " Anima naturaliter christiana," in : NCE 1 : 545.
[16] On this see : J. Gross, op. cit., 70-111.
[17] Cf. A. Strucker, *Die Gottebenbildlichkeit des Menschen in den ersten zwei Jahrhunderten.*

tracted from the transcendence of God, who is portrayed as holy and heavenly in His inaccesible majesty. Therefore the similarity of man to God is limited by God's transcendence and to His authority corresponds man's dependence and obedience.

In this context we have to take a closer look at the narrative of the fall of man contained in Gen 3,1-24. Usually this text is interpreted in a sense that the devil in the guise of a serpent tempted man to abandon as insufficient the idea of his similarity to God and to strive for equality with God in dignity, authority and full autonomy. This form of titanism, it is said, constituted the essence of original sin and was the cause of the fall of man.

This interpretation in view of biological evolution and biblical investigation of the images contained in Genesis does not hold ground any more. According to the more recent interpretation the serpent is a remnant of the mythos of the primordial dragon which is the symbol of life and existence.[18] Man, therefore, is in constant struggle with life and in constant process of falling and rising again. His situation is ambiguous or even contradictory and his salvation is in God, who by His grace and friendship makes man similar to Himself. God grants man the means of transcending himself and of becoming God-like, that is divinized and capable of sharing in God's intimate life, light and love.

Old Testamental anthropology has many examples of this sharing of man in God's personal life, light, love, or even power. Thus the ascensions of Henoch and Elias (4 Kings 2,1-14) are images of the possibility offered to man to rise to the realm of God and to be welcomed into His most intimate and mysterious friendship. The figure of Moses, the transmitter of the Law, is the image of man sharing in the divine power to teach and to rule. The prophets are inspired to speak to Israel in the name of Yahweh. By this they were made divinized partakers in the mysteries of the divine knowledge and the message of salvation. The whole people of God as a corporate personality was constantly summoned to holiness and righteousness, that is to divinized existence in the friendship of God and man. The pinnacle of this tradition is to be found in Psalm 81,6 f : " You are gods, and all of you, the sons of the Most High.7.Yet, like men you shall die,

---

[18] Cf. R. C. Zaehner, *Matter and Spirit. Their Convergence in Eastern Religions, Marx and Teilhard de Chardin* (Harper and Row, New York and Evanston 1963) 44-67 ; Fritz Buri, *Der Pantokrator. Ontologie und Eschatologie als Grundlage der Lehre von Gott* (Herbert Reich, Hamburg-Bergstedt 1969) 56-64.

and you shall fall like anyone of the princes." Other texts in the Old Testament which are presented as the foundation of the doctrine of the divine sonship of man are to be found in the Book of Wisdom 2,23-25 ; 3,1 ; 5,27, etc.

The inter-testamental period witnessed certain struggle sinvolving two trends of anthropological thought. In Qumrān we find side by side statements concerning the exaltation of man and his lowliness and sinfulness.[19] However the Qumrān tradition always interpreted the Torah as a summons to perfection. The rabbis of the period on the other hand minimized the importance of Torah and expanded their casuistry in which there was no room for the divinization of man or the theophany of God. Fortunately Philo of Alexandria re-discovered the idea of divinization of man and later on exercised an important influence on patristic thought.[20]

However the *theosis* of man and of the cosmos is an idea primarily to be found in the New Testament. The distance between God and man was conquered by the God-man and the only mediator Jesus Christ. In His person he conquered not only the moral abyss that separates a sinful being from God, but also the distance between the infinite God and the finite man. According to St. Paul it was God's initiative without human collaboration which revealed to men salvation in Jesus Christ and made it accessible to man through faith in Him. St. Paul was the first to reflect on the distinction between divinization and deification even if this terminology is not to be found in his writings. In his famous discourse in the Areopagus in which he quoted Cleanthes (Acts 17,28-29) St. Paul taught : " 28.For in him (i. e. God) we live and move and have our being, as indeed some of your own poets have said, *For we are also his offspring.* 29. If therefore we are the offspring of God, we ought not to imagine that the Divinity is a thing of gold or silver or stone, an image graven by human art and thought."

Besides we find the foundation for the doctrine of *theosis* in St. Paul's mysticism, in his anthropology, soteriology, ecclesiology and in his teaching on the Eucharist and Baptism.[21] According

---

[19] Cf. I QH III, 19 ff. On the tradition of Qumranic dualism cf. J. Edgar Bruns, *The Art and Thought of John* (Herder and Herder, New York 1969) 100.

[20] Cf. J. Pascher, Ἡ βασιλικὴ ὁδός. *Der Königsweg zur Wiedergeburt und Vergottung bei Philon von Alexandreia* (Paderborn 1931).

[21] Cf. Alfred Wikenhauser, *Die Christusmystik des Apostels Paulus* (Herder, Freiburg i. Br. 1956²) ; Lucien Cerfaux, *Christ in the Theology of St. Paul* (Herder, Freiburg i. Br. 1962) 365-534.

to St. Paul each of the faithful through baptism enters into an objective and subjective Christ-event which tends towards the final fulfillment (Rom 6,4-10 ; Phil 3,12). Through Baptism the faithful are buried with Christ so that they can also live together with the resurrected Christ in the new life (Rom 6,4-11). The eternal life of the faithful begins with Baptism but reaches fulfillment after the Resurrection of the dead, through which the whole person of man is mysteriously reconstituted and transformed by divine *dynamis* into incorruption, glory, power and a spiritualized body (I Cor 15,44ff). In Philippians 3,20-21 he says : " 20. But our citizenship is in heaven from which also we eagerly await a Saviour, our Lord Jesus Christ, 21. who will refashion the body of our lowliness, conforming it to the body of his glory by exerting the power by which he is able also to subject all things to himself."

The above statement of St. Paul introduces us to a new dimension of the eschatological divinization, namely to the divinization of the whole cosmos. One of the most explicit texts illustrating this mystery is Rom 8,18-22. The crucial v. 21 reads : " ... creation itself also will be delivered from its slavery to corruption into the freedom of the glory of the sons of God." Other relevant biblical texts concerned with the mystery of the divinization of the cosmos are : Isa 65,17 ; 66,22 ; 2 Pet 3,10-13 ; Apoc 21,1ff ; Mt 24,1-25,46.

The idea of divinization or *theosis* is clearly outlined in 2 Pet 1,3-4 where the participation in divine power is portrayed as the highest gift of God which makes it possible for the faithful to escape the destructive pleasures and desires of this world and to become partakers in the divine nature. In 2 Pet therefore the idea of *theosis* is not yet fully developed, especially in view of its negative attitude towards the world.

A much more precise idea of *theosis* is to be found in the Synoptic Gospels, e. g. Mt 5,1ff ; 25,31ff ; Mc 1,14ff ; Lk 15,1ff. The images employed here are those of the divine adoption and of the participation in the Kingdom of God or the Kingdom of heaven. The " *metanoia* ", faith and love of God and of all men are portrayed in the Synoptics as the necessary prerequisites to these higher and divine goods.

The teaching of *theosis* enters into a new phase of development through the writings of St. John, where it receives a very special mystical Johannine trait.[22] The Incarnation of the Logos

---

[22] R. Schnackenburg, *Joannes-Briefe* (Freiburg i. Br. 1963[2]) 66-72.

opened to the faithful a new source of the highest goods and graces which are summed up in the eternal life which is given here and now to the well disposed faithful of Christ the Lord (John 1,1ff, 3,15ff).[23] Through love and the Sacraments, and especially through the Eucharist, the faithful are mystically united to Christ and through Him to God (Jo 4.15ff : 3,5 ; 6,32ff ; 17,1ff). Thus for St. John union with Christ is a necessary bridge to union with God. He is very careful to avoid anything that would suggest deification of man, and therefore he distinguishes quite clearly between the unity of the Father and the Son and the union between God and creatures, especially man. Therefore only Jesus can say " I and the Father are one " (Jo 10,30). Man on the other hand must use other formulas, e. g. " fellowship ... with the Father, and with his Son Jesus Christ " (1 Jo 1,3) ; or " But he who keeps his word, in him the love of God is truly perfected ; and by this we know that we are in him " (1 Jo 2,5) ; or : " Whoever confesses that Jesus is the Son of God, God abides in him and he in God " (1 Jo 4,15), etc.

These and other formulas of reciprocal immanence do not spell out identity, but a real unity of being and life, which is open to all in Jesus and which is the eternal life in us here and now, and the warrant of eternal life in the final and eternal fulfillment and fellowship with God. In other words God's personal authority as Creator and Lord and His eschatological salvific and gracious activity, which mystically transfigures and mysteriously transforms creatures and creates a dynamic tension between the present and the future eternal life, light and love, is of the essence of *theosis*.

In the same sense, i. e. in the sense of *theosis*, we have to interpret other important New Testament terms and statements which on the one hand indicate a new mode of being of the creature and on the other hand express precise ethical imperatives, e.g. to be born of God (1 Jo 2,29), the children of God, new birth or re-birth, *metanoia*, transfiguration, to put on Christ (Gal 3,27), which indicates a sharing in the mode of existence of Christ, the new man (Eph 4,24) which connotes the winning back of the primordial image of God which was given to us in creation, and such profound descriptions as in 2 Cor 3,18 : " But we all with faces unveiled, reflecting as in a mirror the glory of the Lord, are

---

[23] Cf. Josyf Slipyj, Die Auffassung des " Lebens " nach dem Evangelium und I Briefe des Hl. Johannes, in : *Bohoslovia* (Rome), XXIX (1965) 2-62 ; reprinted in : *Opera Omnia Card. Josephi (Slipyj Kobernyckyj-Dyckovskyj) Archiepiscopi Maioris* (Romae 1968) 31-90.

being transformed into his very image from glory to glory, as through the Spirit of the Lord."

From this biblical evidence it is sufficiently clear that the doctrine of *theosis* as presented by the Greek Fathers, and generally in Eastern liturgies, is not merely a philosophical speculation or a product of the pagan mythologies which by the process of osmosis penetrated Christianity. It is in fact a biblical and divinely revealed mystery which is presented to us in an unprecedented number of images and which seems to constitute the very essence of Christian anthropology. On the other hand, *theosis* is closely related to the religious experience of men of all times and as such constitutes the necessary foundation for an inter-faith dialogue.[24]

Theosis in the teaching of the Eastern church fathers [25]

St. Ignatius of Antioch continued to develop the biblical tradition of realized eschatology and to present salvation as a sharing in the divine life, light and love. He coined many beautiful words, which, unfortunately, fell into oblivion and are not the object of theological reflection today, e. g. θεοφόροι (carriers of God) χριστοφόροι (carriers of Christ), ἁγιοφόροι (carriers of sanctity).[26] As yet St. Ignatius did not use the term *theosis* but no doubt the content of this doctrine is quite clearly developed in his symbolic language.

The II and the III centuries witnessed bitter fights between traditional Christianity and Gnosticism, which reduced redemption to a mere re-divinization of the divine germ in the pneumato-

---

[24] Up until now there has been an apologetic effort on the part of many authors cited in this paper attempting to prove that Christian *theosis* has absolutely nothing to do with pagan deification. However this view must be corrected.

[25] Besides J. Gross, op. cit., 116-351, see : V. Ermoni, " La deification de l'homme chez les Pères de l'Eglise ", in : *Revue du clerge français* 11 (1897) 509-519 ; L. Baur, " Untersuchungen über die Vergöttlichungslehre in der Theologie der griechischen Väter ", in : *Theologische Quartalschrift* (Tübingen), 98 (1916) 467-491, 99 (1918) 225-252, 100 (1919) 426-446, 101 (1920) 28-64, 155-186 ; M. J. Congar, " La deification dans la tradition spirituelle de l'Orient," 'n : *Vie spirituelle*, supplement, 43/2 (Avril-Sept. 1935) 91-107 ; A. Festugière, " Divinisation du Chrétien ", in : *Vie spirituelle*, Supplement 59 (1939) 90-99 ; H. Rondet, " La divinisation du chrétien " : *Nouvelle Revue Théologique* 71 (1949) 449-476, 561-588 ; G. van Randenborg, *Vergottung und Erlösung* (Berlin, no date) ; Irénée-H. Dalmais, " Divinisation (II. Patristique Grecque) " : *Dictionnaire de Spiritualité* (Paris 1957) III, 1376-1389.

[26] Eph. 9,2.

phores or pneumatics, who were considered by the Gnostics to be the only true Christians. Against these aberrations the Apologists raised their voice, defending the traditional Christian theology of hope, which teaches that salvation is accessible to all and not to the chosen few. Besides they taught that the eschatological incorruptibility of the whole human being is rooted not in the nature of man, but in the divine grace and a participated immortality in the immortality of God, who is immortal by nature. And thus according to Theophilos of Antioch, who incidentally was a resolute enemy of philosophy, an immortalized man by the grace of God can be called " proclaimed God " (θεὸς ἀναδειχθείς).[27]

However the first writer to give us a consistent and highly developed doctrine of *theosis* was St. Irenaeus.[28] In his classic work *Adversus haereses* in the introduction to the Fifth Book he says : " Deus Logos factus est quod sumus nos, ut nos perficeret esse quod est ipse." (P. G. 7,1120). " God the Logos became what we are, in order that we may become what He himself is." Following evidence found in the New Testament St. Irenaeus also taught that *theosis* was envisaged by God at the moment of creation as the final goal of man. For St. Irenaeus also the beatitude of immortality is simply a prolongation of that divine life which we possess in this world as the result of our union with Christ and with the Holy Spirit. He rejected the idea of magic re-divinization of some spiritual seed in the pneumatics taught by the Gnostics, and defended our likeness to God, which is the result of the indwelling of the Logos and of His Spirit. For Irenaeus both the Incarnation and the death of the Lord Jesus have equal value for our redemption. He first established the foundation for the *anakephalaiosis* or the recapitulation of the whole extra-divine reality in Christ.[29] Out of it flows the re-unification in Christ of all men, who, having received in Him access to God, are blessed with immortality and likeness to God. This was the first attempt to outline the physical theory of divinization.

The same ideas we find in the writings of Methodios[30] and

---

[27] Theoph. Ad Autol., II, 24.

[28] Cf. M. Aubineau, " Incorruptibilité et divinisation selon Saint Irénée " : *Recherches de science religieuse* 44 (1956) 25-52.

[29] Cf. R. Haubst, Anakephalaiosis : *LThK²*, I, 466-467 ; G. A. Maloney, *The Cosmic Christ from Paul to Teilhard* (Sheed and Ward, New York 1968) 107-110 ; E. R. Carroll, " Recapitulation in Christ " : New Catholic Encyclopedia (New York, etc 1967) 12 : 126-127.

[30] Cf. J. Gross, *La divinisation du chrétien d'après les pères grecs* (Paris 1938) 191-200.

Hippolytos [31] and in the Alexandrian School, especially in Clement [32] and Origen.[33]   At that time the School of Alexandria had to face a serious threat — Gnosticism.   In order to defeat this error on its own ground, Clement and Origen christianized the Greek ideal of the assimilation of man to God by means of knowledge (*gnosis*) and asceticism.   Here are visible very strong neo-Platonic and encratic tendencies.   The true *gnosis* consists in the perfect understanding of the heavenly doctrine revealed by the incarnate Logos. This *gnosis* which involves the whole man, is a result of both human effort and the grace of God.   This *gnosis*, which is the contemplation of the supreme being, assimilates man to God, who is the source of all perfection, and confers upon man impassibility, immortality, wisdom, and love.   According to Clement this type of Christian *gnosis* " divinizes " or even " deifies " the Christian, and he was the first to use this term in a verb form.

According to the School of Alexandria the pinnacle of divinization here on earth is to be seen in the ecstatic union of a mystic and gnostic with God.   In opposition to the neo-Platonic *gnosis* this Alexandrian type of *gnosis* was not conceived as a union or divinization which identified the gnostic with God, therefore it was not a deification properly so called, even if an improper term θεοποίησις (deification) was employed in this instance.   The proper term " *theosis* " or divinization came into use at a later date.

This type of *theosis* was too intellectualized, but it had a salutary effect, because from now on Christian *gnosis* or faithful knowledge came to be considered along with the idea of incorruptibility as the constitutive element of *theosis*.   Therefore it prepared the way for the classical formulation of the doctrine which was spelled out by Athanasius the Great (295-373) : " Αυτὸς γάρ (ὁ τοῦ θεοῦ Λόγος) ἐνανθρώπησεν, ἵνα ἡμεῖς θεοποιηθῶμεν." " For He (the Word of God) became man, that we may become gods." [34]

In order to avoid possible misinterpretations of this classic statement, which exercised tremendous influence on later patristic thought, it is necessary to present a few quotations from the writings of St. Athanasius [35] which would illustrate his theological

---

[31] Ibid., 186-191.
[32] Ibid., 159-174.
[33] Ibid., 174-185.
[34] De Incarnatione 2,54 : P. G. 25, 192.
[35] K. Bornhäuser, *Die Vergottungslehre des Athanasius und des Johannes Damascenus* (Gütersloh 1903) ; J. Roldanus, *Le Christ et l'Homme dans la Théologie d'Athanase d'Alexandrie* (E. J. Brill, Leiden 1968).

Weltanschauung and would serve us as a theological background of that period.

First of all St. Athanasius speaks very clearly of the unity and harmony of the natural and supernatural cosmos, a vision dear to many Eastern Church Fathers : " Like a musician who has attuned his lyre, and by the artistic blending of low and high and medium tones produces a single melody, so the Wisdom of God, holding the universe like a lyre, adapting things heavenly to things earthly, and earthly things to heavenly, harmonizes them all, and, leading them by His will, makes one world and one world-order in beauty and harmony " (Contra Gentes, 41).

However St. Athanasius leaves no doubt as to the Pantocratic function of Christ in this unified world-vision : " ... but, because He is good, He guides and settles the whole Creation by His own Word, who is Himself also God, that by governance and providence and the ordering action of the Word, Creation may have light, and be enabled always to abide securely. For it partakes of the Word who derives true existence from the Father, and is helped by Him so as to exist, lest that should come to it which would have come, but for the maintenance of it by the Word, namely, dissolution, — ' for He is the Image of the invisible God, the first-born of all Creation, for through Him and in Him all things consist, things visible and things invisible, and He is the Head of the Church ' (Col 1,15-18), as the ministers of truth teach in their holy writings " (Contra Gentes, 41).

Also St. Athanasius was quite explicit concerning the divinization of Creation and its union with God the Father, through the Son (Logos) and in the Holy Spirit : " When the Logos descended into the Holy Virgin Mary, the Spirit came at the same time into her, and in the Spirit it is that the Logos was formed and His body was adopted, wishing through Him to unite and offer the Creation to the Father " (Ad Serapionem, I, 31).

" It is then in the Spirit that the Logos glorifies Creation and deifies it and adopts and conducts it to the Father. But He who unites Creation to the Logos would not make a part of the created world just as He who confers filiation upon creatures would not be a stranger to being a Son. If such would be the case, one must search for another Spirit because in the first Spirit man is united to the Logos. This, however, is absurd. The Spirit does not make part of created things, but is proper to the divinity of the Father and it is in Him that Logos deifies the creatures " (Ad Serapionem, I, 25).

From these texts it is clear that St. Athanasius is one of the chief exponents of the spiritual optimism of the Christian East. It is also clear that he means *theosis* or divinization whenever he uses the term *theopoiesis* or deification. It must also be borne in mind that the writings of St. Athanasius and especially his teaching concerning *theopoiesis* should be understood against the background of the Arian crisis in which the divinity of the Logos was put in question. To him the Logos is God because if He were not, He could not divinize us and the cosmos.

From the teaching of St. Athanasius we can deduce three principal moments in the doctrine of *theosis* : firstly the deification of the human nature in the God-man Jesus Christ ; secondly, and as the result of the first moment, the divinization of the whole person of a Christian ; thirdly as the result of the first two moments, the divinization of the whole cosmos. All three moments of *theosis* constitute the central part in the dogmatic system of St. Athanasius and occupy the most prominent place in the Greek patristic teaching on redemption. Let me enumerate the most important representatives in this area : St. Gregory of Nazianzus,[36] St. Basil the Great,[37] who however was very cautious in his presentation of *theosis*, St. Gregory of Nyssa,[38] and especially St. Cyril of Alexandria, who probably represents the pinnacle in the development of teaching on *theosis*.[39] In the period of the first attempts at a synthesis of earlier patristic thought we see the teaching on *theosis* embedded in the expositions of Pseudodionysios the Areopagite,[40] Maximus the Confessor [41] and John of Damascus.[42]

In the rival school of Antioch this idea survived, as it seems since the time of St. Ignatius, despite the rationalist currents which characterize the thought of this school. Here the most important exponents were St. John Chrysostom [43] and Theodoret.[44]

It is true that we find no separate treatise on *theosis* or *theopoiesis* in the Greek Fathers or Eastern Fathers in general.

---

[36] P. G. 35, 397-400 ; 785 ; 36, 101, 321-324, 325 ; 37, 957.

[37] P. G. 39, 665.

[38] P. G. 45, 52, 65-68 ; 44, 1317-20.

[39] P. G. 73, 160 ; 74, 280, 785-788 ; 75, 1081, 1084, 1089. Cf. J. Mahé ' La sanctification d'après saint Cyrille d'Alexandrie," in : *Revue d'histoire ecclesiastique* 10 (1909) 30-40, 469-492.

[40] P. G. 3, 373-376, 424.

[41] P. G. 90, 400-401, 449, 520 ; 91, 33-36, 404.

[42] P. G. 39, 665.

[43] P. G. 59, 93 ; J. Gross, op. cit., 253-262.

[44] P. G. 83, 177. Theodoret even uses the term " *theopoiesis* ".

But this does not detract from the fact that this doctrine was central to their view, deeply embedded in their speculations and mystic perception and one which was put forth quite naturally almost by all of them. Analogically in that time we have no systematic treatise on the Church, but this does not mean that the reality of the Church did not constitute an important object of their theological view or that it was not part of their daily Christian existence and experience. Patristic piety, liturgical hymnology and theology are deeply permeated and profoundly influenced by the doctrine of *theosis* or *theopoiesis*, and it constitutes one of their distinctive characteristics.

The Christological disputes of the IV to VIII centuries produced many important by-products. One of them was a clarification of the doctrine of *theosis*, e. g. Anastasius of Sinai (VII century) in his polemical work against monophysite understanding of the deification of the human nature in Christ taught : " *Theosis* consists in elevation to the higher, and by no means in the suppression or change of the nature." This statement he defends in the following terms :[45] " Divinized means that something has been elevated to a higher splendor, and not that it was emptied of its nature." Translated into our modern terminology this means that in the process of *theosis* the human person is divinized, that is assumed into the higher and internal life of God, and by no means de-humanized or bereft of its human qualities and properties. On the contrary, concomitant to divinization is the process of true humanization, because man comes closer to God the Omega, God the Fulfiller, the ground of being and perfection and therefore comes closer to the real self.

Starting from the XI century on until the end of the XV century there is a certain revival of the doctrine of *theosis*. The chief exponents during this period were Simeon the New Theologian († 1022), Nicholas of Mathone († 1165), and especially Gregorios Palamas whose writings initiated the famous Palamitic or Hesychast controversy. Since that time *theosis* became one of the most cherished expressions of Eastern Christian spirituality.[46]

The third revival of this doctrine can be observed in contemporary Orthodox (especially Russian and Greek) theology, e. g. Lot-

---

[45] P. G. 84, 77.

[46] Cf. Panagiotis Bratsiotis, " Die Lehre der Orthodoxen Kirche über die Theosis des Menschen ", in : *Mededelingen van de Koninklijke Vlaamse Academie voor Wetenschappen, Letteren en Schone Kunsten van België. Klasse der Letteren* XXIII/1 (Brussel 1961) 1-13.

Borodine,[47] A. Theodorou,[48] S. Zankov,[49] J. Karmiris,[50] P. Trembelas,[51] P. Evdokimoff,[52] and especially Panagiotis Bratsiotis, who in describing the essence of the *theosis* of man says : " The meaning of this *theosis*, of this deification, is the elevation of the human nature into the sphere of the divine and its spiritual, mystical union with God. The main moments of this *theosis* are for the body the conquest of the material element, the spiritualization, the incorruptibility and immortality ; for the soul — the spiritual, mystical transformation and union with God through his grace."[53]

The above description is reflecting the traditional Greek theological terminology. Some of its elements are evidently not consonant with modern philosophical and theological experience. However this in itself does not invalidate the teaching of *theosis* and its necessity for modern man. On the contrary it should serve as an invitation to further study and updating of this important doctrine.

Theosis and Western Christianity [54]

Western theological tradition by recognizing Christological diophysitism of the Council of Chalcedon in fact accepted the doctrine of *theosis* of the human nature in the God-man Jesus Christ. However, Western Christian tradition did not accept the term " theosis " or its equivalent for the description of that mystery and the predominant term became "incarnation"; even if it is not the best one there is, e. g. *"enanthropesis"* or "inhominization" seems to be much more exact.

As far as the *theosis* of man is concerned, that is the mystery of salvation and glorification of man wrought in Jesus Christ, Western theology, especially since the XII century, tended to

---

[47] M. Lot-Borodine, " La doctrine de la déification dans l'Eglise Grecque jusqu'au XI siècle," in : *Revue de l'histoire des religions* (Paris) 105 (1932) 1-43 ; 106 (1932) 525-574 ; 107 (1933) 8-55.

[48] A. Theodorou, *The Doctrine of the Greek Church Fathers until John of Damascus on the Theosis of Man* (Athens 1956). In Greek.

[49] St. Zankow, *Orthodoxes Christentum des Ostens*, 57 ff.

[50] J. Karmiris, *Die Orthodoxe Kirche in griechischer Sicht* (Stuttgart 1959) I, 53 ff.

[51] P. Trembelas, Δογματικὴ τῆς ὀρθοδόξου καθολικῆς ἐκκλησίας (Athens 1959) II, 116 ff. ; (Athens 1961) III, 494 ff.

[52] P. Evdokimoff, L'Orthodoxie (Neuchatel, Paris ; 1959) 93-97.

[53] P. Bratsiotis, op. cit. in note 46, p. 7.

[54] On history of theosis in Western Christianity see article " Divinisation ", in : *Dictionnaire de Spiritualité* (Paris 1957) III, 1389-1459.

23

emphasize the removal of sin and the reparation or redemption. Thus instead of the Eastern theology of *theosis* there appeared in the West the doctrine of grace. The preferred terminology was "adoption", "regeneration", "new life", "reparation" etc. However, there were notable exceptions, e. g. Tertullian [55], St. Augustine [56], St. Hilary of Poitiers [57], St. Bonaventure [58] and St. Thomas Aquinas [59], who under the influence of the Greek Fathers and especially of St. John of Damascus and Nemesius used also the term "deificare" in order to explain the ultimate effect of grace. Recently the interest in this doctrine seems to be growing in the West.[60]

As the time passed by the differences between Eastern and Western Christian approaches to the mystery of salvation and grace were becoming more and more diverse, because respective developments, terminologies and points of emphasis were receiving their distinctive Eastern or Western shape. However, the substance of the doctrine of salvation and grace remained the same in both the East and the West. In other words Christian theology taught the supernatural and sanctifying grace, the new life in Christ resulting from it, the participation in the mystical body of Christ and the indwelling of the Trinity in the faithful Christian.

Just the same, in the East the doctrine of *theosis* remained the focal point of the doctrine of salvation and the doctrines of sanctification by the Holy Spirit, of the glorification of man and of the resurrection of the whole man in body and soul never lost

---

[55] Tertullian used the term "deificus" in a sense of "divinized" : Apologeticum 11,10 : P. L. 1, 335a, cf. 11, 1-2 : P. L. 1, 332a-333 a.

[56] St. Augustine besides using the term "deificus" used also such terms as "deificor" (Ep. 10,2 : P. L. 33,74), "deificatus" (Sermo 166,4 : P. L. 38, 909) in a sense of *theosis*. Cf. P. Dumont, "Le surnaturel dans la théologie de Saint Augustin," in : *Revue des sciences religieuses* 12 (1932) 55. J. A. A. Stoop, *Die Deificatio hominis in die sermones en epistulae van Augustinus* (Leiden 1952) ; V. Capanaga, "La deificación en la soteriología augustiniana," in : *Augustinus Magister* (Paris 1954) II, 745-754.

[57] Ph. T. Wild, *The Divinization of Man according to St. Hilary of Poitiers* (Mundelein 1950).

[58] J. Hartnett, *Doctrina S. Bonaventurae de deiformitate* (Mundelein 1936).

[59] Cf. *Summa Theologiae* I-II, q. 112, a. 1c, and I-II, q. 3, a. 1 ad 1.

[60] Besides literature listed above cf. : W. T. Witley, *The Doctrine of Grace* (London 1932) ; F. Walland, *La grazia divinizzante* (Asti 1949) ; V. Rüfner, "Homo secundus Deus", in : Philosophisches Jahrbuch 63 (1955) 248-291 ; A. Piolanti, "La Grazia come participazione della Natura Divina," in : *Euntes Docete* 10 (1957) 34-50 ; M. Schmaus, *Katholische Dogmatik* (München 1965⁶) III/2.

their vigor and freshness as was the case in the West. Here, the doctrine of grace became a highly rationalized portion of dogmatic theology which soon degenerated into the polemical theological issue which is known as the famous controversy between the schools of Bañez and Molina concerning sufficient and actual grace. Besides, the sanctification of the human soul alone was overemphasized to the detriment of the correct Christian view of the unity of man or better the totality of his person.

The whole situation became extremely complex during the Lutheran Reformation. Here the doctrine of justification assumed the dominant position, which it was never meant to occupy. Besides it was accompanied by an extreme theological and anthropological pessimism according to which man's nature, because of the original sin, is totally corrupt and permanently sinful to such an extent that it remains in sin even after the justification, because sins are not really forgiven but only forgotten by the merciful God on account of their being covered by the merits of Christ.[61] Evidently in this doctrine of the non-imputation of sins there was no room for a real ontological change of man as the result of a real forgiveness of sins. There was no room for a real inner " *metanoia* " of a sinner accompanied by a new life, transfiguration, sanctification by the Spirit and *theosis* with all its constitutive moments.[62]

On top of that there emerged a rugged individualism in the theology of grace which culminated in the questions concerning the individual predestination and the efficacious and sufficient grace of the individual Christian. The sight of the collective or ecclesial and cosmic aspect of grace was almost completely lost, evidently

---

[61] The young Luther as far back as 1518 in his " Probationes Conclusionum " of the Heidelberg dispute taught in Probatio XIII : " Prima pars patet, quia est captivum et servum peccato, non quod sit nihil, sed quod non sit liberum, nisi ad malum." His pessimism concerning the ontological and ethical dignity of man is clearly stated in Probatio IIII : " Quod cum agnoscimus atque confitemur, nulla in nobis est species neque decor, sed vivimus in abscondito Dei (id est in nuda fiducia misericordiae eius)."

[62] It is important to note that according to the Eastern Christian theology, the Incarnation means an ontological (i. e. physical and appropriate to human nature and being) superelevation, which, however, must also express itself ethically. Therefore good deeds of man are a *conditio sine qua non* of divinization. Thus a moral life and divinization are the two inseparable poles of Redemption. If one of them is given up, the whole structure necessarily collapses. Thus divinization entails very many existential, moral, ontological, interpersonal and inter-Personal implications, as well as inseparable unity of ontology and ethics. Cf. P. Evdokimov, *L'Orthodoxie* (Neuchatel, Paris 1959) 93-97.

to the detriment of the correct Christian understanding of created reality, ecclesial reality and divine self-revelation.

It is my contention that the contemporary theology is desperately searching for a new and refreshing avenue to be followed. Theologies of humanization, action, revolution, hope, temporal values, etc., as well as de-mythologization, re-mythologization, de-hellenization, etc., are indeed symptoms of this search. It seems that the sooner the whole of Christianity regains the biblical and theological tradition of *theosis*, the better for the renewal of Christianity and even for the progress of mankind as a whole because modern man needs firm hope and a positive approach to contemporary and eschatological reality. All sciences and human efforts, and especially theology and anthropology, must end in eschatological doxology of God, God-man, man, and the cosmos, because otherwise they will remain sterile and incredible to the modern man.[63] The right step in this direction was made by Teilhard de Chardin in his writings in which divinization was integrated into hominization and humanization in the personalized universe.[64]

Theosis and mysticism [65]

Serious study of the mystery of *theosis* could contribute new insights into the nature of mysticism. The notion of mysticism in many instances is overhastily identified with unusual phenomena such as ecstasy, stigmatization, levitation, etc., or is simply described as follows: " (a) an experience, the interior meeting and union of a man with the divine infinity that sustains him and all other being — in Christian mysticism, in Judaism and Islam, with the personal God — as well as (b) the attempt to give a systematic exposition of this experience, or reflection upon it (hence a scientific ' discipline ')." [66]

However, the true nature of Christian mysticism can be grasped

---

[63] On Eastern Christian eschatology see : G. Florovsky, " Eschatology in the Patristic Age " : Studia Patristica, Vol. II, Texte und Untersuchungen zur Geschichte der altchristlichen Literatur (Berlin 1957), Vol. 64, pp. pp. 235-250 ; C. Callinicos, *Beyond the Grave : An Orthodox View of Eschatology* (Scranton, Pa. 1969).

[64] Cf. Ladislaus Polgar, *Internationale Teilhard Bibliographie 1955-1965* (Freiburg/München 1965).

[65] Cf. on this V. Lossky, *The Mystical Theology of the Eastern Church* (London 1957) ; Idem, *The Vision of God* (London and Clayton, Wisc., 1963).

[66] K. Rahner - H. Vorgrimler, *Theological Dictionary* (Herder and Herder, New York 1965) 301.

only in the context of the *theosis* of man and the whole visible and invisible cosmos. In fact, true Christian mysticism is a new and divinized relation of the whole man to the totality of reality including God and the visible and invisible cosmos. This means that a true, genuine, and full Christian mysticism is not a transitory experience. On the contrary, it is a permanent Triadic mysticism in that God's inner Triadic life, light, and love is communicated by Christ the All-Ruler and in the Holy Spirit to the individual and to the community, who experience this divine, loving, and condescending activity and respond by acts of faith, hope, and love. This is achieved especially by communal liturgy,[67] ascetic purification and renunciation, and Christian involvement in the world, because genuine Christian mysticism is not a denial but a contemplation of the world as a divinized creature of God and of the transfiguratory effort in it. This type of mysticism, therefore, presupposes a rejection of meeting with the eternal and infinite All. It is also a denial of monism, and pantheism. Yet it is not a rejection, but an acceptance of a natural mysticism, which is an experience of a transcendence or self-transcendence of man toward the absolute, the eternal, and the infinite. Mysticism, therefore, is one of the expressions of *theosis* and as such is closely related to it. It could be viewed as a road or means to the definitive eschatological *theosis* of man and the world. Thus, we must conclude that mysticism without *theosis* is neither really logical nor theologically defensible.

Theosis and realized eschatology

Realized eschatology as it is taught today in scholarly circles can be summed up as follows :[68] In the earliest Christian tradition

---

[67] I stress very much the communal aspect of mysticism despite the fact that it is usually denied, e. g. K. Rahner and H. Vorgrimler, *Theological Dictionary* (Herder and Herder, New York 1965) 301 : " Mystical contemplation, submerging the soul in ˉits source, is always the act of the individual, not of the community of worshippers : but the individual may have mystical experience during worship." It is my contention that Eastern liturgies in general are directed toward and animated by the communal mystical experience and that an individual mystical experience is primarily an extension of the communal.

[68] An outstanding representative of this thought is C. H. Dodd, *The Parables of the Kingdom* (London ; Fontana Books, 1961) ; Idem, *The Interpretation of the Fourth Gospel* (Cambridge, 1963) ; Idem, *Historical Tradition in the Fourth Gospel* (Cambridge 1963). Also J. Edgar Bruns, *The Art and Thought of John* (Herder and Herder, New York 1969) gives

Jesus was understood to have proclaimed that the Kingdom of God, the hope of many Old Testament generations, had at last arrived. This was understood as a new covenant or as a fulfillment of the historical expectations of Israel expressed by the prophets. The contemporaries of Jesus in fact could see and know God in Jesus Christ and through the Spirit. Christ is the *eschaton*, or the divinely ordained climax or crisis of history. He came as a gift of God and not on account of human effort. It was the manifest and effective assertion of the divine sovereignty in conflict with evil in the world. This assertion became manifest in the effective " signs " and teaching of Jesus and in His gift of " eternal life ". The eternal life, light, and love brought by Jesus, which are perpetually present in the Church and in its Sacraments, constitute the eternal life, light, and love which are released from their limitations and which are experienced as changing human beings and their inter-personal relationship.

Realized eschatology, therefore, contradicts in many points the speculations of the apocalyptic writers with their descriptions of future cataclysms after which the Kingdom of God or of heavens would come. The essence of the gospel then as seen in the context of a realized eschatology is the proclamation of the Kingdom of God who manifests Himself in the crucified, risen, and exalted Christ the Lord, who in the Spirit here and now communicates to men the eternal life, light, and love of the Triadic God.

It is necessary to admit that the re-discovery by the biblical scholars of a realized eschatology is one of the greatest achievements in modern exegesis. However, this achievement remains incomplete because as yet there is no serious study on the relationship between a realized eschatology and *theosis*. As I pointed out above, the teaching on *theosis* is a legitimate successor, so to speak, to many New Testament expressions and ideas, which constitute the essence of the Christian message concerning man and the cosmos in relation to God. Therefore, the doctrine of *theosis* is a systematized theological elaboration of the biblical data including realized eschatology. I hope that a systematic theological elaboration of the relationship between the teaching on *theosis* and realized eschatology will produce many new and fruitful results not only for the purely theological investigation of the mystery, but also for the renewal of Christianity and of the whole human society.

---

an excellent account of the doctrinal and historical background of the realized eschatology of St. John.

The doctrine of *theosis* is also very valuable to those theologians and philosophers of religion who do not admit the exisence of the immortal human soul, the doctrine of resurrection or immortality, but who do admit the existence of a personality established in faith, which continues to exist after death with God, who is conceived not as a being but as presence. In fact, this type of thought would profit very much from the doctrine of *theosis*, because it would give to it greater consistency by expressing *theosis* as the only lasting gift, i. e. the process through which the above mentioned personality in faith is being established and the final eschatological fulfillment or state in God.

Conclusion

In closing, let me state that the idea inherent in *theosis* of " one world and one world order in beauty and harmony ",[69] which is the work of the divine wisdom, could help modern Christians to bury the hierocracy, exaggerated sacralism, clericalism, ecclesiasticism, sacramentalism, papocaesarism and caesaropapism, Manicheism, and pessimism of the past which assumed the total corruption of man after original sin. It could also help to overcome contemporary errors such as exaggerated secularization, secularity and secularism, as well as atheistic and agnostic humanism, religious indifferentism, Pelagianism or Semi-Pelagianism, and exaggerated humanistic optimism. In my opinion, all these errors were rooted in the misunderstanding of the most basic Christian message : Emmanuel, or " God with us ", that is God who creates, loves, attracts, vivifies, enlightens, strengthens, illumines, purifies, redeems, sanctifies, re-unites, resurrects, assumes, transfigures, glorifies His creatures or simply the one who divinizes them because of His condescension and their humanizing co-operation.

Institute of Christian Thought
University of St. Michael's College

---

[69] St. Athanasius, *Contra Gentes*, 41.

the Christology of Teilhard de Chardin

Originally published in the *Proceedings of the Teilhard Conference 1964* (New York: Fordham University, n.d.), pp.109-133. Reprintrd here with permission.

The Christology of
Teilhard de Chardin

Petro Bilaniuk

SPEAKING OF THE place of Christ in his evolutionary *Weltan-schauung*, Teilhard says:

> Christ coincides (not withstanding its deepening still) with what I have called above the Omega point.
> Christ consequently possesses all the superhuman attributes of the Omega point.
> These two propositions resume in my mind the passionate expectations and advances of our Chistology which are already in progress.[1]

The above text, as well as a number of others that could be cited, witness to the Christocentricity of Teilhard's thought. So strong is this accent, that his entire position and system stands or falls with his belief in Christ, the cosmic Pantokrator, the Omega point, who gives his unified vision its consistency, meaning, and foundation, as well as constituting its ultimate end. Therefore, it is my contention, perhaps exaggerated, that only a good theologian with a solid scientific and philosophical background, can understand the ultimate implications of Teilhard's thought.

However that may be, it is undeniable that the vast majority of Teilhard's theological works focus on Christology. The others contain so many Christological references **that** they can be viewed as Christological corollaries.[2]

---

[1] "Super-Humanité, Super-Christ, Super-Charité," (1943) in IX, 209. (Translations are the author's.) Karl Adam remarked correctly that "our entire religious position stands and falls with the belief in Christ," *The Christ of Faith* (New York: Random House, The New American Library, 1962), p. 18. This, in a much higher degree, is true of Teilhard's position, because of his striking Christocentricity.

[2] Cf. Claude Cuénot, *Pierre Teilhard de Chardin* (Paris: Plon, 1958), Premier essai de bibliographie, pp. I-XLI.

Further, of all the neologisms Teilhard created, and here he is probably next in line to Tertullian, the founder and inventor of Latin theological terminology, the most numerous, most striking, most exact and all-embracing are Christological coinages.[3] It is, indeed, possible to feel in all his works that everything he does or says, and the reality he comes in contact with, bears a Christological seal and dimension. All his paleontological works, for example, are nothing else than a study of a particle of the Christogenesis or the Christosphere. They serve the one main purpose of showing or substantiating a direction in the general drift of the universe, evolution's striving toward its ultimate goal, the Omega point, or the universal and cosmic Christ in his Pleroma.

This tendency goes so far as to lead Teilhard to postulate a third, "cosmic," nature in Christ, which seems to have a universal extension, which touches, penetrates, and almost absorbs all created reality, serving as its main unifying, natural, and supernatural principle. It is for this reason that any treatment of the place of Christ in Teilhard's system involves all other theological areas of consideration. And it is for this reason, therefore, that in treating of Teilhard's theology, we have chosen to treat primarily of his Christology.

GENERAL QUESTIONS CONCERNING TEILHARD'S CHRISTOLOGY

1. On the general characteristics of Teilhard's Christology

For the time being it is very difficult to speak authoritatively of Teilhard's Christology. We do not yet possess the necessary prerequisites, for example, a critical edition of all his works in chronological order, with exact indexes and bibliographical notes. What is possible are only provisory and superficial sketches, outlines, and remarks.[4] Teilhard does not, of course, attempt to construct a

---

[3] Almost any term Teilhard uses has a remote Christological dimension, but of 383 terms listed by C. Cuénot (*Lexique Teilhard de Chardin*) at least 45 are directly Christological. A profounder investigation of Teilhard's terminology and neologisms is badly needed.
[4] During the elaboration of this paper I learned that Fr. Christopher Mooney, S.J., submitted a doctoral dissertation in theology on the Christology of Teilhard de Chardin at the Institute Catholique in Paris. [Soon to be published by Collins (London) and Harper (New York) under the title *Teilhard de Chardin and the Mystery of Christ. Ed.*]

coherent Christological treatise. We can describe his Christology as an analysis of certain points of the Christological dogma and the mystery of Christ with a definite outline of a far-reaching and all-embracing synthesis.

His is in fact a classical example of *fides quaerens intellectum*, one which respects the deposit of faith, and yet draws from it "new things and old." In his prophetic, scientific, and theologico-mystical vision,[5] Teilhard perceived the truth, strength, and beauty of the divine revelation of the mystery of Christ, as well as of the most classical pronouncements of the Church's magisterium. He does not challenge the traditional Christological fundaments, does not refuse to accept traditional Christological doctrine. On the contrary, he appeals constantly to the authority of the Sacred Scriptures and the Tradition of the Church to substantiate his Christological claims. Teilhard did not, understandably enough, possess a detailed knowledge of the development of the Christological dogma, because in his time this question was still rather obscure.[6] However, he has a very acute sense and a vivid perception of its existence and necessity.[7]

Respectful of the past, therefore, Teilhard is also acutely aware of the spiritual and material needs of modern man and is not afraid to speak to him in present day scientific language, thereby performing simultaneously the prophetic, scientific, and apologetic functions.[8] He exhibits, moreover, an unparalleled awareness of the mystery of our faith called "Jesus the Christ": for him it is the most life-giving, life-explaining, life-consuming, and all-embracing principle in all its supernatural, natural, metaphysical, mystical, and cosmological aspects and dimensions. This mystery embraces

[5] On the "concordism" danger skirted here, see below, pp. 120 ff.

[6] It was only towards the end of Teilhard's life that such works appeared as A. Grillmeier, S.J., and H. Bacht, S.J., eds., *Das Konzil von Chalkedon: Geschichte und Gegenwart* (Würzburg: Echter Verlag): I. Der Glaube von Chalkedon (1951), II. Entscheidung um Chalkedon (1953), III. Chalkedon heute (1954). Of special interest to Teilhard would have been Allan Galloway, *The Cosmic Christ* (London: Nisbet and Co., Ltd., 1951).

[7] E.g., in his *Le Christique* (unpublished; New York, March 1955), Teilhard states: "Now, on the contrary, when by all the paths of experience the Universe has begun to grow so fantastically before our eyes, the time has certainly come for Christianity to awaken to a distinct consciousness of the hopes raised by the dogma of Christian Universality, transposed to these new dimensions,—and conscious, at the same time, of the difficulties it stirs up."

[8] Cf. C. D'Armagnac, "La pensée du P. Teilhard comme apologetique," *La Nouvelle Revue Theologique*, LXXXIV (1962), 598-621.

and explains the whole man and the totality of the extra-divine, created, cosmic, and evolving reality, and constitutes the final cause which gives them their ultimate meaning and fulfillment.[9]

Christology is a term, therefore, which for Teilhard looks into both past and future. To the past, because it implies the unique divine revelation of the mystery of Christ in the setting of the other mysteries of our faith; to the future, because it implies that our faith involves subjective progress, supposing a homogeneous evolution of Christological dogma along lines both traditional and new. This renewal and advance of traditional Christology is for Teilhard a necessity of our times, as well as a source of joy and optimism for the future, because in all this he perceives the realization of his "passionate expectations."

While fully accepting the Christological formulations of the past, however, Teilhard is led in many instances to underline their incompleteness, especially in the cosmic and cosmological dimensions.[10] Therefore we can detect in his works polemic overtones directed against those who would restrict the meaning and cosmic extension of Christ's influence. His main intention is not polemic, however; it is scientific and apostolic. As a mystic of Christ, he feels an urge to communicate his inner experience, to show its relevance to the world about him. Thus, he seems to be an outstanding representative of the new twentieth century interpretation of the mystery of Christ, one of the most unique personalities in the mysticism of Christ. All this makes him an important figure in that effort toward a quanti-

---

[9] This is evident from one of the most classical Christological texts of Teilhard found in *Comment je crois* (unpublished; Peking, 28 October 1934): "Under the combined influence of science and philosophy, the world more and more impresses itself upon our experience and thought as a system linked together by an activity gradually rising higher and higher toward freedom and consciousness. The only satisfying interpretation of this process is to regard it as irreversible and convergent. Thus ahead of us lies a clearly defined *universal cosmic center* to which everything leads and in which everything is self-explanatory, conscious and self-controlled. In my opinion, it is in this physical pole of universal evolution that the plenitude of Christ will be located and recognized. And this because *in no other kind of cosmos* and *in no other place* could a being, *no matter how divine*, exercise that function of universal consolidation and universal animation which the Christian dogma ascribes to Jesus. In other words, Christ must be at the summit of the world if He is to consummate it, just as He needed a Woman for His conception." Text cited by Claude Tresmontant, *Pierre Teilhard de Chardin, His Thought* (Baltimore: Helicon Press, 1959), p. 71.

[10] This is clear from all the works of Teilhard, especially *Le Milieu Divin*.

tative and qualitative growth in our subjective penetration of Christian revelation, which is implied in the notion of dogmatic development.[11] As a contribution to this development, Teilhard's Christology is necessarily bound to the time-space continuum and its circumstances, indeed, even the solemn definitions of the Church do not wholly escape this fate. At the same time it seems sure that certain elements in Teilhard's Christology cannot be ignored by any serious theologian simply because of their dangerous quality, for example, the "third Christic or cosmic nature" in Christ. Nor may we discard those other elements which have every chance of surviving the vicissitudes of the time-space continuum to become incorporated into the universal Church's Christological doctrines. Among these latter we may note the unity of the entire cosmos in Christ, the Christocentricity and Christoformity of all creation, which Teilhard sets forth in unheard of strength, realism, and beauty. A modern man of tremendous all-sided interests, he has, as a believing Christian, asked the very important existential question, of how each particular dogma of faith influences our lives, which mystery of faith it expresses, and what its significance is, for both the concrete individual, human society, and for the whole extra-divine reality.

The most interesting and important points in his Christological texts are: the coincidence of Christ with the Omega point, his reference to a third cosmic nature in Christ, and the new Christological vision, or better, the outline he presents of a future Christology's structure, one which implies a very basic rethinking and reinterpretation of the coherence and interdependence of such fundamental mysteries of faith as God, Creation, Incarnation, Redemption, and Consummation.

Teilhard's unified vision of the cosmos is therefore Christocentric in the eminent sense of the word. We could even term it a "Christosophy" because of its very striking intermarriage between the Greek Christian "sophia" with its inherent mystical realism, and the modern existential and Christian vision of the whole natural and supernatural reality. The first of these elements prompted him to try to transcend all scientific, philosophical, and theological categories, not by denying them, but by integrating, coordinating, and subordinating them into one Christian vision. The second aspect helped him to see the mysteries of our faith not only as a set of dogmatized propositions (all too often, alas, isolated from concrete supernatural and living

---

[11] For some good bibliography on this question, consult K. Rahner, "Dogmenentwicklung," *Lexikon für Theologie und Kirche*, III, 457-463.

reality) but as dynamic, living, and life-giving, penetrating created reality both in its totality and in the diversity and individuality of its parts. Thus his Christosophy helps him to view everything in the natural and supernatural order as the gift of God or divine grace, something which he presupposes everywhere.[12] This in turn helps him to avoid the danger of theological rationalism, which tries to convert the mysteries of our faith into a system of scientific or philosophical propositions. All this explains why Teilhard's religious appeal has begun to reach great proportions, penetrating not only scientific, philosophical, and theological worlds, but also the highest levels of the Church's magisterium, for example, pontifical documents such as *Pacem in Terris* and the preparatory schemata of the Second Vatican Council.[13]

2. On the principles underlying Teilhard's Christology

Teilhard's evolutive *Weltanschauung* perceives the whole cosmos in a constant drift of development towards higher and higher forms culminating in man, and by prolongation in the absolute, hyperpersonal, and all-embracing Omega point, which he identifies with Christ or with God. Therefore for him the two principles *omnia propter hominem*[14] and *omnia uni* complement and fulfill each other on one natural-supernatural plane unified by God.[15]

This brings us to the realism, naturalism, and cosmological accent in Teilhard's theological thought. This is a feature which is being

---

[12] In the Preface to *The Divine Milieu* (New York: Harper & Row, 1960), p. 12, Teilhard writes: "Nor should the fact arouse concern that the action of grace is not referred to or invoked more explicitly. The subject under consideration is actual, concrete, 'supernaturalized' man—but seen in the realm of *conscious* psychology only. So there was no need to distinguish explicitly between natural and supernatural, between divine influence and human operation. But although these technical terms are absent, the thing is everywhere taken for granted. Not only as a theoretically admitted entity, but rather as a living reality, the notion of grace impregnates the whole atmosphere of my book." Cf. H. de Lubac, *La pensée religieuse de Père Teilhard de Chardin* (Paris: Aubier, 1962), pp. 174-175.

[13] *Pacem in Terris* of John XXIII (11 April 1963) seems to have been written under the influence of Teilhard. Some of the Schemata prepared for the third session of Vatican II (e.g., "On Original Sin") are strongly Teilhardian.

[14] *La Vision du Passé* (Paris: Editions du Seuil, 1957), p. 189.

[15] See H. de Lubac, *La pensée religieuse du Père Teilhard de Chardin* (Paris: Aubier, 1962), pp. 169-183.

minimized by his friends in order to save him,[16] and rejected outright by his enemies.[17] However, a closer scrutiny of the situation reveals an underlying fear of all these people not to violate the divine transcendence by exaggerating the divine immanence in the world and its different parts.[18] They think that by minimizing immanence they will preserve transcendence. However, is it not possible to say that immanence and transcendence complement each other on the part of the absolutely simple pure act of the subsisting existence itself, the ground of being, that is God? How this is possible remains an obscure and impenetrable mystery into which, however, we can get some modest insight. By denying formally and materially all sorts of pantheism and by affirming the infinite immanence of God in the created extra-divine reality, we are affirming divine transcendence, or at least we are pointing out one of its aspects, because it is true to say that God is so perfectly and infinitely transcendent, that even his infinite immanence does not diminish it, but on the contrary heightens it.

It was said a long time ago that God is more present to creatures than creatures can be present to themselves. It is equally true, that the heightening of the creature's presence to God, and by the same token the heightening of God's immanence to the creature, does not destroy the individuality, liberty, being, personality, or any other property of the creature. On the contrary, it heightens them, because the heightening of the closeness to God is an expression on the part of the creature of its transcendence, or self-transcendence: it comes closer to itself in coming closer to the ground of all being, God himself.

God is transcendent not only because he stands infinitely above, apart, and outside created, finite, and relative extra-divine reality, but also because he can by his infinite immanence penetrate, put-himself-in-the-presence-of, sustain, govern, this extra-divine reality to such an infinite extent, that on the one hand he does not destroy created beings, and on the other hand "immanates" them so infinitely that he reaches into the core of their existent being to spheres where

---

[16] Cf. Alois Guggenberger, *Teilhard de Chardin: Versuch einer Weltsumme* (Mainz: Grünewald, 1963), pp. 84-85.

[17] See Joseph Meurers, *Die Sehnsucht nach dem verlorenen Weltbild: Verlockung und Gefahr der Theses Teilhard de Chardins* (München: Anton Pustet, 1963), pp. 93-112.

[18] On the immanence and transcendence of God, see: Michael Schmaus, *Katholische Dogmatik* (München: Hueber, 1962), II/1, 109, also 41 (Bibl.).

they are no more and where he alone, the infinite God, can extend
his infinite transcendence. Humanly and figuratively speaking, God
is infinitely transcendent not only towards the "above," but also
towards the "below": "within" and "through" creatures. In other
words God is infinitely transcendent not only in what is customarily
described as his transcendence but also in what is customarily described as his immanence. Therefore we can call God the para-immanent, trans-immanent, or hyper-immanent ground of being. As a
consequence, any attempt at minimizing his immanence is at the
same time an attempt to minimize his transcendence. In the light of
this attempt to clarify the idea of God's immanence, many of Teilhard's expressions and his whole orientation toward matter become
much clearer. Teilhard loves matter precisely because to him, as to
any believing Christian, it is a "diaphany of God":

> If we may alter a hallowed expression, we could say that the great
> mystery of Christianity is not exactly the appearance, but the transpa-
> rence, of God in the universe. *Yes, Lord, not only the ray that strikes
> the surface, but the ray that penetrates; not only Your Epiphany, Jesus,
> but Your Diaphany.*[19]

Matter is an outstanding part of "the divine milieu." As a creature
of the Trinitarian God it carries the trinitarian seal upon itself, the
seal of a natural obediential potency to become supernaturalized
or divinized:

> I salute thee, divine Milieu, charged with Creative power, Ocean
> turbulent with the Spirit, Clay moulded and animated by the Word
> incarnate.[20]

Many of Teilhard's words and texts speak of matter in the religious
and theological realm and dimensions.[21] By far the most important,
though, are those with a definite Christological reference, for example:

> In our hands, in the hands of all of us, the world and life (*our world,
> our life*) are placed like a Host, ready to be charged with the divine
> influence, that is to say with a real Presence of the Incarnate Word.
> The mystery will be accomplished. But on one condition: which is that

[19] *The Divine Milieu*, p. 128.
[20] "La puissance spirituelle de la matière" (written in Jersey, 8 August 1918),
Hymne de l' Univers (Paris: Éditions du Seuil, 1961), p. 73.
[21] See note 2, page 109, above.

we shall believe that this has the will and the power to become for us the action—that is to say the prolongation of the body of Christ.[22]

For Teilhard there is also a "prodigious identification of the Son of Man and the divine *milieu.*"[23] In much stronger language he says: "Quite specifically it is Christ *whom we make or whom we undergo in all things.* Not only *diligentibus omnia convertuntur in bonum* but, more clearly still, *convertuntur in Deum* and quite explicitly, *convertuntur in Christum.*"[24]

All these texts retain their theological validity as excellent mystical illustrations of the immanence of God and of Christ in the concrete world we are living in, and of the divinizing activity we witness to in our faith. With such a high esteem for matter, it is no wonder that Teilhard is extremely optimistic concerning the whole evolutive process and especially its last stage of convergence on the Omega point:

In effect, since ultimately all things in the Universe are moved towards Christ the Omega; since all cosmogenesis, including Anthropogenesis, is ultimately expressed in a Christogenesis; it follows that, in the integrity of its tangible layers, Reality is charged with a divine Presence. As the mystics sense and portray it, everything becomes physically and literally lovable in God; and reciprocally God becomes knowable and lovable in all that surrounds us. In the greatness and depths of its cosmic stuff, in the maddening number of elements and events which compose it, and in the fullness of the general currents which dominate and set it in motion like a great wave, the World, filled with God, no longer appears to our opened eyes as anything but a milieu and an object of universal communion.[25]

Another important passage reads:

For if truly, in order that the Kingdom of God may come (in order that the Pleroma may close in upon its fulness), it is necessary, as an essential physical condition, that the human Earth should already have attained the natural completion of its evolutionary growth, then it must mean that the ultra-human perfection which neo-humanism envisages for Evolution will coincide in concrete terms with the crowning at the

---

[22] *The Divine Milieu*, p. 128.
[23] *Ibid.*, p. 111.
[24] *Ibid.*, p. 112.
[25] "Super-Humanité, Super-Christ, Super-Charité," (1943), IX, 213.

Incarnation awaited by all Christians. The two vectors, or components as they are better called, veer and draw together until they give a possible resultant. The supernaturalized Christian Upward is incorporated (not immersed) in the human Forward! At the same time Faith in God, in the very degree in which it assimilates and sublimates within its own spirit the spirit of Faith in the World, regains all its power to attract and convert![26]

Many modern thinkers, even some outstanding and world-famous minds, are suspicious of, unhappy about, or even hostile to the use of universal evolution in the explanation and faithful penetration of the divinely revealed truth about the mystery of Christ or any other mystery of our faith. The reason for this is a struggle between the static and fixed on one hand and the dynamic and evolutive idea of the world on the other hand, and between mentalities carrying them. The static and fixist mentality is suspicious of the dynamic and evolutive mentality, because it thinks that the latter is always a total destruction of all stability, immutability, and transcendence of both the natural and the supernatural truth. And we have to admit that for untrained minds this is indeed a real danger.

However, it is entirely wrong to ascribe to Teilhard an evolutive mentality which is dominated by the dynamic, mobile, instable, and relative ideas only. But let us turn our attention to the idea of truth and its correspondence to reality in Teilhard's thought.[27] Generally speaking, he was a realist, who trusted his senses and his inner mystical perception dominated by love, and who at the same time believed in the divinely revealed truth and its stability, especially

---

[26] "Le cœur de problème," *L'Avenir de l'homme* (Paris: Éditions du Seuil, 1959), p. 348. On p. 347 we read: "Par habitude, nous continuons à penser et à nous représenter la Parousie (par quoi doit se consommer le Règne de Dieu sur Terre) comme un événement de nature purement catastrophique, c'est-à-dire susceptible de se produire sans relation précise avec aucun état déterminé de l'Humanité, à n'importe quel moment de l'Histoire. C'est un point du vue. Mais pourquoi, en pleine conformité avec les nouvelles vues scientifiques d'une Humanité en cours actuel d'Anthropogénèse, pourquoi ne pas admettre plutôt que l'étincelle parousiaque ne saurait jaillir, de nécessité physique et organique, qu'entre le Ciel et une Humanité biologiquement parvenue à un certain point critique évolutif de maturation collective?" Attached to this text is the following footnote: "Et en parfaite analogie, ajoutons, avec le mystère du premier Noël qui n'a pu s'opérer (tout le monde est d'accord là-dessus) qu'entre le Ciel et une Terre *prête* socialement, politiquement et psychologiquement à recevoir Jésus."

[27] Cf. H. de Lubac, *La pensée religieuse du Père Teilhard de Chardin*, pp. 249-266.

because of the universal activity and stability of the Omega point. His whole transcendent world, God, the Cosmic Christ in his Pleroma or the Omega Point, exhibits an absolute stability. From the psychological point of view we can say that one of his main preoccupations was precisely to search for and to find the consistent, immutable, and absolute reality beneath and within the veil of the evolutive cosmos. In this respect the following illustration may be helpful: the Old-Church-Slavonic language and those affiliated with it (like Ukrainian and Russian) distinguish between *pravda* and *istina*, both of which in all translations mean, unfortunately, "truth." The difference between these, however, is profound. *Pravda* is a human, changeable, relative, and rather weak truth, is exposed to the vicissitudes of the time-space continuum and of the limited human being. In its present state it is a weak, temporal, and limited icon of *istina*, the divine, immutable, absolute and infinite truth. Neither of them may be thought of as terms and concepts belonging to the semantic and logical order only, for according to the original Old-Church-Slavonic usage they are primarily realities belonging to the ontological order. This precisely brings these concepts very close to Teilhard's realism. At the same time the two belong to the same complex of mysteries as the coexistence of God and the creature, infinite and finite, eternal and temporal, absolute and relative, a complex which cannot adequately be explained by weak human terms.

Now applying the *pravda-istina* category to Teilhard's Christological thinking, we arrive at the following picture: Christ as the eternal Logos of God the Father is *istina* only. But as the incarnate Logos he reveals *pravda* characteristics also, that is, in his human nature, he is subject to the same laws and evolutive process as the cosmos itself. Both on the natural human level and in the mystical sphere he is being born, lives, dies, develops, grows, and transfigures himself. Because he is *pravda* he can redeem and through himself reunite the extra-divine *pravda* with the eternal and divine *istina*. He himself is both. Translated into more technical theological terminology, Christ, the Cosmic Pantokrator, redeems and leads all created extra-divine reality through himself and in the Holy Pneuma to God the Father, conducting it from the outer to the inner sphere of the Triadic God's life and love.

Thus it is illegitimate to accuse Teilhard, as some do, of subjecting not only Christ, but also the Triadic God himself in his transcendence to the evolutive process and of consequently destroying the concept of *istina* in the divine realm; according to Teilhard, Christ became *pravda* in the human and cosmic dimension precisely to grant us an access to the eternal and absolute *istina*. Much of this can be found in this profound text of Teilhard:

> Since Christ was born, since he has ceased to grow, since he is dead, *everything has continued to be moved, because Christ has not yet finished forming Himself.* He has not gathered to himself the final fold of his Robe of flesh and love, by which his faithful form him. *The mystical Christ has not attained his full growth, nor hence has the cosmic Christ.* At the same time *they both are and are becoming,* the one and the other; and in the prolongation of this begetting is placed the ultimate mainspring of all created activity. Christ is the goal of the Evolution of beings, even the natural evolution of beings; evolution is holy.[28]

3. On Teilhard's Christological Method

Teilhard's method of Christological research and presentation is not always the same, not always of a single type. He does not study or portray Christology in all its details, but he does study and tries to predict in all its details the universal cosmic evolution. At times, accordingly, he takes this evolutive *Weltanschauung* as his point of departure and tries to bring new insights into Christological dogma as expressed by the magisterium of the Church. His love for the world and for matter, make him try by his mystical experience and perception to penetrate still deeper into the divinely revealed mystery of Christ.[29]

At other times he travels in the opposite direction: starting from the mystery of Christ, he tries to view all created reality from the Christological point of view.[30]

At still other times he seems to be moving in a mystical vision in both directions at once, thereby achieving such a striking, profound, and unified vision of divine and created reality and of their meeting point—the Cosmic Christ—that even a trained and open-minded theologian is sometimes unable to grasp the totality of his vision.[31]

This complex method has not infrequently been called a superficial concordism,[32] a forceful stretching and abuse both of the divine

---

[28] "La vie cosmique" (24 March 1916), *Hymne de l' Univers*, p. 144.
[29] E.g., this is true of Teilhard's *Phenomenon of Man.*
[30] Cf. "Le Christique."
[31] This is at least partly true of *Le Milieu Divin.*
[32] Teilhard himself (in a short paper referring to himself in the third per-

data of revelation and the results of the ever changing natural sciences, in order to bring them to a unique harmony and matching vision. But Teilhard is, in fact, far removed from such illegitimate attempts to investigate Holy Scripture and its divine message for scientific, philosophical, or for any other type of knowledge, which it is not meant to provide. He does not confuse forms of knowledge taken from different sources, or mix principles and methods peculiar to each order of knowledge or research. His method is a subtle and complex penetration of the mystery of Christ by the use of the evolutive *Weltanschauung* as the legitimate tool. Modern Christians are not scandalized when they investigate the works of the Fathers of the Church who use Platonic and Neo-Platonic principles of philosophy to penetrate and explain the data of the divine revelation, nor by the medieval and scholastic theologians, who used Aristotelian philosophy to do the same thing. They read with equanimity the works of modern theologians who use, sometimes quite successfully, the principles of existential philosophy in their theologizing. Yet they seem to be very upset when Teilhard uses this evolutive *Weltanschauung* for the same end.

Teilhard's Christology reveals, as we have said, occasional polemic overtones, because all his life he was fighting against the extreme theological view, based on false philosophical speculation and the underdeveloped exegesis of his time, that the evolutionary mentality and the doctrine of evolution itself were diametrically opposed to the divine revelation and the dogmas of the Catholic Church. But he had to fight another extreme as well, an anticoncordist reaction which went beyond the limits of its own purpose. In answer to the accusation that Teilhard "confuses planes that should be kept separate," Claude Tresmontant has described this view in the following terms:

> The anticoncordist reaction—legitimate in itself—has engendered an aberration-in-reverse which may be formulated as follows: there is no

son) thus explains this difficulty: "this 'philosophy' has been reproached as being only a generalized concordance. To this criticism Père Teilhard responds that one must not confuse concordance with coherence. Religion and Science represent, in the mental sphere, two different meridians which it would be false not to separate (a concordist error). But these meridians must meet at some place on a pole of common vision (coherence); otherwise everything breaks up in us in the domain of Thought and Knowledge." "La pensée du Père Teilhard de Chardin," *Les études philosophiques,* Nouvelle Série, 1955, No. 4, 581.

intelligible relation between the real (creation such as it appears to us) and the Word of God, and this to such a degree that one might ask whether, indeed, it is the same God who is the author of the one and the other.

Instead of making a clear distinction between these domains, which is legitimate, the anticoncordist reaction has separated them. This makes the relation between the world and the Word of God unintelligible. The final outcome is an incoherent pluralism of "visions of the world": the biblical, the scientific, the philosophical, and (why not?) the esthetic, etc. In the modern world the *homo biblicus* appears like a ghost.[33]

Special Questions Concerning Teilhard's Christology

1. On the third christic or cosmic nature in Christ

According to Teilhard the whole cosmos in all its parts and phenomena can, for a believing Christian, become a prolongation of the Body of Christ: Christ can be seen and touched in all things by the faithful.[34] Such statements can be understood only in view of the cosmic dimension taken on by the person of Jesus Christ, the point which became one of the major cornerstones of his outlook. His mystical reflections about this cosmic dimension of Christ gave rise, however, to some statements concerning the third christic or cosmic nature in Christ, and these in turn became major targets of his enemies and a source of embarrassment to his friends.[35]

The first of his statements is found in the unpublished essay "Comment je vois," § 31, written in August 1948. He writes of

... a renewed Christology, which reveals itself as an axis, not only as a historic or juridical, but as a structural axis, of all theology. Between

[33] *Pierre Teilhard de Chardin, His Thought*, p. 69.
[34] Cf. notes 19 to 24.
[35] E.g., Teilhard's "anonymous" enemy in *L'Osservatore Romano*, Édition Hebdomadaire en langue Francaise, No. 28 (656), 13 July 1962, p. 7, wrote the following accusation: "In the essay already quoted, *Le Christique*, is written bluntly—it is said 'in a true meaning'—a 'third nature' of Christ, not human, not divine but 'cosmic'. We do not wish to take to the word 'in a true meaning' what Teilhard writes on this point, otherwise it would be a veritable heresy. But such statements, evidently, add to a confusion of ideas which is already considerable."
Pierre Smulders, *Theologie und Evolution* (Essen: Hans Driewer Verlag, 1963), p. 304, n. 263, speaks of "jene schokierende dritte, kosmische Natur Christi."

the Word on the one hand and the Man Jesus on the other, a sort of christic 'third nature' (if I may say so!...) emerges—we can read of it everywhere in the writings of S⁺. Paul: the whole Christ, who unifies and in whom, because of the transforming effects of the resurrection, an individual human element born of Mary has been found elevated not only to the state of the cosmic Element (or Milieu, or Curvature), but also to the ultimate psychic center of the universal assemblage.

The second text is found in one of his last works, "Le Christique" (unpublished; written in New York, March, 1955).

> ... All Christian tradition is unanimous, in the total (whole) Christ there is not only man and God, but there is also him who, in his theandric being, resumes and reassembles all Creation: *in quo omnia constant.* Up till now and despite the dominant place that St. Paul gives it in his vision of the world, this third aspect or function—or even in a true sense, this third "nature" of Christ, a nature neither human nor divine but "cosmic," has not as yet attracted much explicit attention from the faithful and the theologians.

It is worthwhile and necessary to subject these texts to an objective and minute scrutiny. First of all neither statement may be taken as an *incidenter dictum.* Both must be considered very seriously because of the quality of the content and of the works in which they occur: the first a sort of profession of his religious and scientific views, the second approaching very closely to a mystical testament.[36]

Secondly, there is an inconsistency observable, even according to the standards Teilhard himself sets, in the use of "christic nature" in the first text and of "cosmic nature" in the second. There is also a difference in intensity of emphasis, the first speaking of "a sort of christic 'third nature' (if I may say so!...)" and the second text alluding to the "third aspect or function—or even in a true sense, this third 'nature' of Christ." Both texts, however, witness to an evolution in Teilhard's Christological views.

Thirdly, a lack of the necessary theological qualifications makes these texts very obscure and extremely difficult to interpret. We

---

[36] The introduction to "Le Christique" begins with the following words: "The pages which follow are not a simple speculative dissertation, exposing the major lines of some system, slowly ripened and ingeniously assembled. Rather do they represent the testimony born, in all objectivity, in a certain interior event, in a certain personal experience where it is impossible for me not to discern the trace of a general impulse of Humanity itself."

do not know, first of all, the sense in which Teilhard used the critical term "nature"; it is well to observe that he placed it in quotation marks in both cases. Whether one regard the Aristotelian[37] or modern existentialist image,[38] the notion regularly implies two distinct but inseparable "moments": a relatively static one, wherein nature designates primarily the essence, the being-thus of the entity in question; and a more expressly dynamic moment, stressing nature as the principle, the norm of the thing's activity. But to add to our confusion, Teilhard generally uses terms like this in a peculiar phenomenological, or at least in a mitigated metaphysical sense, with a very strong phenomenological connotation. Besides, in his "Le Christique" he most probably used the term in a sense neither metaphysical nor phenomenological, but in a mystical sense which mediates and transcends them both, raising both of them to a different order on the basis of his mystical perception. Such a term can contain many subjective and unexplainable elements and aim remotely at illustrating rather than at scientifically expressing the mystery of being concerned. Besides we have to keep in mind, that in all Christological definitions the word "nature" is used analogically, it expresses something *simpliciter diversum et secundum quid idem* in each case when applied to God and to man, because it would be a heresy to claim that the word "nature" is equivocally or univocally applied in both cases.

Aside from the term "nature," however, there are other obscurities in these texts. We do not know, for instance, what Teilhard understood by the term "theandric being." There is no specification concerning the relationship of this "third nature" to the hypostatic union, to the *constitutivum formale* of the hypostatic union, etc. We do not even know whether he conceived this "third nature" as being in union strictly *in persona et ad personam Verbi* or as a nature attached to another intermediary nature and through it with the person of the Logos. Another possibility is that Teilhard had in mind a "third nature" which stands between the human and divine natures and binds them somehow together. All these possibilities are open.

One solution which is to be rejected: as an argument that would lessen Teilhard's guilt in his lack of precision, it might be said that

---

[37] Cf. M. Schmaus, *Katholische Dogmatik* (München: Hueber, 1963), § 146 (cf. also §§ 39 and 58).
[38] Cf. K. Rahner and H. Vorgrimler, *Kleines Theologisches Wörterbuch* (Freiburg i. Br.: Herder, 1962), p. 255.

a theoretical theological consideration could claim that it is non-repugnant to the infinite Person of the divine Logos, or to any of the Persons of the most holy Trinity, to be united hypostatically to an indefinite number of finite natures. It might be suggested that knowing this, Teilhard may well have thought that Christianity was not yet explicitly aware that revelation implied a third nature in Christ, and that it was high time to investigate its possibility, to bring it into the open and draw all its practical consequences for the benefit of our mature Christian existence. From this standpoint the texts above might be interpreted as a *status quaestionis* to a possibility of the third nature in Christ and not as affirmation of its factual existence. It is far more probable, however, that Teilhard was convinced that, if the faithful and theologians were to investigate the sources of divine revelation concerning Christ, this would certainly lead to the dogmatization of the "third nature" he alludes to here.

Teilhard's probable meaning: he quite clearly thought that Christ's cosmic primacy had, up to the time of his writings, been regarded from the outside and described in juridico-moral terms only: to illustrate and partly explain its significance as a reality, he thought, one had to adopt an evolutionary interpretation of the world. The root of this mistake was probably his training in a rather formalistic scholastic theology and philosophy, and his lack of acquaintance with the neo-scholastic research and progress made by more recent theology. He seems to have underestimated the fact that St. Paul, St. John, the Fathers of the Church, and many modern theologians arrived at the cosmic importance of Christ in complete ignorance of any evolutionary *Weltanschauung*, or of his "third christic or cosmic nature."[39]

His phenomenological and evolutionary *Weltanschauung* having led him, therefore, to perceive very vividly the dynamic moment of nature, and somewhat more obscurely its static moment, his mystical perception detected Christ's strong cosmic influence and activity, indeed, the Christo-formed and Christo-centric quality of all created extra-divine reality. As a consequence, we may think, he overhastily concluded to a third cosmic nature of Christ, thus

---

[39] Cf. Allan Galloway, *The Cosmic Christ* (London: Nisbet & Co., Ltd. 1951); M. J. Scheeben, *Die Mysterien des Christentums: Gesammelte Schriften* (Freiburg: Herder, 1958), II, pp. 260-384; M. J. Scheeben, *Handbuch der Katholischen Dogmatik*, V/1 Erlösungslehre: Gesammelte Schriften VI/1 (Freiburg: Herder, 1954).

departing from the more correct position expressed in *The Divine Milieu*.

He seems to have been unaware that the theology of the Fathers of the Church, as well as the whole tradition which culminated last century in Joseph Matthias Scheeben,[40] tried to demonstrate how Christ possessed his pantokratic and cosmic primacy over the universe precisely in virtue of his true and integral humanity. This primacy is realized in the overflowing of fullness and perfection, only possible in the case of the God-man, on account of his universal theandric activity, with no need of appealing to some third cosmic nature. As first-born of all creatures, Primate, Lord, and Head of all Creation, he possesses absolute and transcendent dominion over the whole cosmos, because he is the Son of Man (John 5:27), and it belongs to the very essence of man to be the pinnacle of the visible creation. Christ is also the redeemer of humanity, because as God-man and in view of the hypostatic union, and his resurrection from the dead, he is the Lord and Master of the whole cosmos and as a consequence the Pantokrator, mighty to conquer all enemies of salvation of the entire cosmos.

To conclude, then, if Teilhard really thought of the third "christic" or "cosmic" nature in Christ in a strict metaphysical sense, which would be really distinct from both the human and divine, something which seems to be improbable, it would evidently be a serious theological error.

Teilhard may not, however, be accused of heresy on this score. The Christological dogma of Chalcedon,[41] of all subsequent councils,[42] and of the ordinary magisterium of the Church, took for their scope only the two natures, divine and human, in complete abstraction from the possibility of a third nature. It was neither proposed, nor challenged, and consequently remained simply outside the scope of Christological dogma. Thus the definition of the two natures in Christ is not synonymous with an automatic exclusion of other possibilities. To make a statement heretical it takes either an explicit and direct opposition to the existing definition of the solemn magisterium of the Church, or a direct contradictory or contrary statement opposing a constant, direct, and explicit teaching or witnessing

[40] Cf. note 39.

[41] H. Denzinger and A. Schönmetzer, *Enchiridion Symbolorum* (Barcinonae: Herder, 1963), 301-302.

[42] *Ibid.*, 553-599 and Ind. syst. E 1a-5b, g.

to the same fact, by the ordinary and daily magisterium. And this is clearly not the case here.

On these, and on so many questions, one can only regret that Teilhard had no opportunity to defend, refine, or retract his contention in scholarly dialogue with the scientific and theological worlds.

We have to keep in mind, finally, that an explanation of the Christological dogma, or of the mystery of Christ, came into existence through the highest authority of the Church, and was prepared by an incredible effort of innumerable doctors and witnesses to Christ. That effort consisted mainly in the fact, that every easy solution was rejected.[43] It is true that only time will show what will happen to Teilhard's "third christic or cosmic nature." As an easy solution to the mystery of Christ the Pantokrator, however, it is destined to die (at least according to my judgment), but its importance will remain as one of the milestones in the history of attempts to explain the cosmic dominion and functions of the God-man, and to guide and form all future theologians.

2. On God's motive concerning the whole extra-divine reality

Christology is, we have said, Teilhard's central theological preoccupation; it is also, for that reason, the door by which he enters into the totality of the theological problematic. This is especially true of the problem we must now consider: the divine motive of creation. For in Teilhard's thought the entirety of the cosmos is viewed as "christic" in all its dimensions, with the result that Creation, Incarnation-Redemption, the final Parousia and Consummation are intricately linked in this regard. Is there, accordingly, some single divine motive for this linked set of Christian mysteries? One which will account for their very linkage, for the very unity of the cosmic process in both natural and supernatural dimensions?

"Motive" is a term which entered the English language through the Old French *motif*, derived from Medieval Latin *motivus* = *moving*, from Latin *movere* = *to move*. Its etymology shows that it connotes a dynamic reality in the line of activity. Webster's defines it as "that within the individual, rather than without, which incites him to action; any idea, need, emotion, or organic state that

---

[43] Cf. P. Smulders, "De ontwikkeling van het christologisch dogma," *Bijdragen* XXII (1961), 357-424.

prompts to an action."[44] In other words, it is that value which moves a freely acting individual to the performance of an act, but which does not compel him to do so. The motive must be carefully distinguished from the formal object, that is, from the very special aspect under which the object is being grasped by an act of the freely moving individual. Sometimes the formal object and the motive can coincide, sometimes not, because the reason why an act is being performed and the chosen aspect of its object can be different. Thus, for example, attrition rejects sin because of the possible punishment (motive), and not as an infraction of God's right concerning man (formal object). Thus, motive and formal object can be two values, the distinction between which does not necessarily destroy the morality of the one unique act.[45]

Now when we speak of any motive on the part of God, it is clear that the "motive" is an analogical term, which must be applied to God with fully conscious rejection of all dangerous anthropomorphisms; no goal, good, or formal object would draw God to itself or move Him from the outside to act. God indeed is the *primus motor immobilis* and cannot be attracted or moved by anything but himself.

Teilhard clearly indicated internal liberty on the part of God as far as the act of creation was concerned,[46] but in his metaphysics of union as applied to the act of creation he seems to have confused the motive and the formal object of creation: God seems to be attracted towards creative union outside of himself.[47] But this apparent error had a very important side-effect: it permitted Teilhard to perceive an inner unity between the different mysteries of our faith,[48] something that must be viewed as a major contribution to contemporary theology.[49] Using Teilhard's principles it would

[44] Webster's New Collegiate Dictionary (Toronto: Thomas Allen, 1949), p. 550.

[45] Cf. K. Rahner and H. Vorgrimler, "Motiv," *Kleines Theologisches Wörterbuch* (Freiburg: Herder, 1963), pp. 249-250.

[46] See the texts of Teilhard in H. de Lubac, *La pensée religieuse du Père Teilhard de Chardin*, p. 282.

[47] *Ibid.*

[48] Cf. texts contained in Pierre Smulders, *Theologie und Evolution*, pp. 168-170 and H. de Lubac, *La pensée religieuse . . .* , pp. 281-295.

[49] E.g., a very strong unitive approach to the different mysteries of our faith can be felt in K. Rahner, "Die Christologie innerhalb einer evolutiven Weltanschauung," *Schriften zur Theologie* (Einsiedeln-Zürich-Köln: Benzinger Verlag, 1962), pp. 183-221, evidently under influence of Teilhard.

be possible to speculate theologically about one unique divine motive concerning the whole extra-divine reality. This motive would be identical with God's absolutely simple nature, and would eliminate anthropomorphic plurality of decrees on the part of God the Creator, Redeemer, Consummator, etc.

First of all let us discuss the motive of the Incarnation. Teilhard is usually classified as in line with the Scotist school on this important issue. But this is only partly true, since he transcends the classical Scotist position in many important features. Karl Adam, whose theological position concerning Christ approaches Teilhard's, deserves quotation in this connection:

> This [i.e., the grounds for the incarnation of the Son] may give us some modest insight into the supernatural motive for the mystery of the incarnation, and into those thoughts of God's that caused Christ to become man. When we speak of Christ's mediation, the first thing that comes to mind is his function of reconciling sinful mankind to God. But this function is only one single impulse in the entire idea of divine mediation. Essentially, it is rather the communication of the marvelous closeness of *God's union with his creation*. And the reconciliation of created beings is only one instance within this. As man, Christ is one with mankind; indeed [one] with the entire created world, at whose head he stands. As God, he stands in a union of substance with his Father, from whom he comes, and with the Holy Spirit, in whom he encounters the Father. Standing in the world, one with the world, he towers up into the very heart of the Godhead, he is God himself, one with the Father and the Holy Spirit. And so in his person, he draws the world up into the very neighbourhood of the eternal Father, while on the other hand he emanates over the entire world the union he has with his Father. He binds God and his creation into such a close reciprocal relationship that he cancels and overcomes not only every abyss of sin between God and his creation but also the infinite disparity that separates them by their very natures; Christ conquers not only religious and ethical remoteness but also ontological distance. The God-man cancels out both the infinite remoteness of sinful being and the infinite remoteness of mere created being. So Christ is the substantial bond which brings together the most disparate antinomies. The Lord's sublime prayer that mankind 'may be one even as we are one: I in them and thou in me; that they may be perfected in unity' is perfectly fulfilled in the God-man (cf. Scheeben, *Mysterien des Christentums*, pp. 350f.)[50]

---

[50] *The Christ of Faith*, p. 238. Original in *Der Christus des Glaubens* (Düsseldorf: Patmos, 1956), pp. 225-226.

Now let us hear Teilhard himself. As far back as 1918 in his essay "L'âme du monde" we read: "While marking a higher stage in the gratuity of the divine operation, are not Creation, the Incarnation, and Redemption each so many acts indissolubly linked in the apparition of participated being?"

In a celebrated passage from "Comment je vois," § 31, 1948, Teilhard is very explicit:

> And thus it is, that step by step, a series of notions viewed for a long time as independent of each other, start before our eyes to bind themselves organically with each other. There is no God (to a certain point . . .) without creative union. There is no Creation without the incarnating immersion. There is no Incarnation without the redeeming compensation.[51] In the Metaphysics of Union, these three fundamental "mysteries" of Christianity do not appear to be more than three faces of the same mystery of mysteries, that is of the Pleromisation (or a unifying reduction of the Multiple).

In a footnote attached to this text we read: "[The above mysteries have been] till now generally presented, I repeat, as entirely separable from each other. In the popular teaching it is still generally admitted: 1) that God could absolutely (*simpliciter*) have created or not created: 2) that if he created, he could have done it with or without the Incarnation: 3) and that if he became incarnate he could have done it with suffering or without it. It is this conceptual pluralism which it appears to me, in all hypothesis, essential to correct."

These texts and many others, usually unpublished and difficult to get,[52] show clearly that it is not permissible to place Teilhard simply in the Scotist Christological tradition. He fights against many of its elements and places it along with other schools in the category of traditional and, in his view, inadequate Christologies. He searches for an inner, ontological nexus between different mysteries of our faith using the principles of his unique metaphysics of union, which is in fact an extreme form of speculative theology. It does not deduce the facts of revelation from the natural sciences and accordingly supply us with what can be called arguments of "convenience" only. His argumentation can be described as follows:[53]

[51] Cf. "Le Christique".
[52] Cf. note 48.
[53] A more complete discussion can be found in Pierre Smulders, *Theologie und Evolution*, pp. 168-177.

When God creates, then he creates a world which evolves from Multiplicity to Unity, a world on its evolutive way from the primitive created "Weltstoff" to God himself. Also implicit in Teilhard's thinking is the conviction that the only possible union with God is grace, which he presupposes everywhere; grace makes man the child of God the Father through union with God the Son, the Incarnate Logos. Theology generally recognizes that union with God consists in adoptive Sonship and that this is the highest form of union. But generally theology is reluctant to recognize this as the only form of union possible, because it is afraid that the gratuity of grace on the part of God would be too dangerously rooted in the fact of Creation. In other words a creature could "demand" the grace of the adopted Sonship, because of the very fact of his existence on account of Creation, and because without this grace, which is rooted in the Incarnation, the creature would be without a real meaning and goal. Teilhard's type of reasoning, therefore, since it oversimplifies the whole picture, tends to destroy the mystery of grace and gives it an explanation which is not acceptable.

His next step, however, is quite correct: the Incarnation of the divine Logos implies necessarily the sacrifice of the Cross, because the Son of God did not accept an abstract human nature, but the one concrete nature of the sons of Adam, which was under the spell of evil and sin. Here he correctly ignores all theological futuribilia of the Thomist and Scotist schools. However, he interpolates strange anthropomorphic elements, namely quantitative and physical concepts; sin and evil, for instance, become almost synonymous with the Multiple, or at least inseparably linked with it. Redemption in consequence, equals unity or unification. But in classical theology and in the words of Jesus, sin and evil are not only an esthetic lack of harmony and unity, but also a real fact of being evil, a profound mystery which cannot be expressed in physico-quantitative terms. Christ did not only carry the burden of the evolution of our love and its disuniting imperfections, but also the burden of our lack of love, of our rebellion and denial of the goodness and rectitude which was manifest in Him. Thus Teilhard's approach is here again an oversimplification: real tensions so visibly manifest in the Bible seem to be toned down too much as well as embedded too deeply in the scientific picture of the world from the first half of the 20th century.

In conclusion, we have to admit that Teilhard's attempt at a theological synthesis of the mysteries of Creation, Incarnation, Redemption, and Consummation contains many elements which are valuable, and extremely important for all future theological work. Let us therefore retain different elements of Teilhard's thought, purified of many excessively anthropomorphic and quantitative features, namely the metaphysics of a free unitive love of God and creatures, one supernatural end of the whole creation in the Triadic God, as well as Teilhard's excellent understanding of the divine immanence and transcendence. Keeping all this in mind, let us, in the light of the Mystery of the Triadic God, search for the one unique motive concerning God's activity to the outside, activity which indeed expresses itself in one eternal plan, one eternal act of love, but to the outside manifests itself in a multiplicity of mysteries, namely in Creation, Incarnation, Redemption, and Consummation, an activity whose motive, I repeat, would coincide with the inner Triadic life and love and reveal to us more or less the following Triadic drama:

Eternity is the mode of existence of God alone. It is one, infinite, internal moment immeasurable and without any succession. In this eternity God the Father, who as head of the Most Holy Trinity neither proceeds, nor is sent, nor is spirated, loves necessarily from all eternity his only begotten Son, the perfect image of Himself, His intellectual emanation, His eternal and divine Logos. God the Father spirates the Holy Pneuma and the Son spirates Him in return. This Holy Pneuma, the third Person of the Most Holy Trinity, is the spirit of love or the inner-divine atmosphere of Love in which God the Father and the Son love each other. God the Father in all eternity is the source of beatitude and love for the Son.

Out of this overflowing love God the Father in sovereign freedom decides to create for his Son in the Holy Pneuma the whole extra-divine reality as an unnecessary, finite, and quasi-additional source of beatitude. He uses as the model his Son, the perfect image of himself and of all creatable things. His decision is creative and because of it He creates through the Son in the Holy Pneuma the whole extra-divine reality. He places it in the outer sphere of life and love of the Triadic God, that is, in the natural sphere, with a destiny to reach him through the Son and in the Holy Pneuma, or better to reach the inner sphere of the divine love and life, that is the supernatural sphere. The whole extra-divine reality moves through the time-space continuum created with it according to the evolutive natural processes implanted in it by the Triadic God. It bears on itself and on all its parts the Triadic and Christological seals, because it is a creature of the Triadic God created according to the image of the incarnate Logos.

This Logos is the real possessor of it. As the real Pantocrator, He unites it to himself, purifies it of sin, redeems it, sanctifies it, and in the Holy Pneuma, the Spirit of Love, graciously through his Pleromisation brings it back to God the Father. He does this, because the whole extra-divine reality is the external source of His beatitude, which reflects to Him the image of His eternal Father and His love for him. He brings it back to the Father in order to enjoy with Him and in the Holy Pneuma its supernaturalized and divinized presence in all eternity, because this extra-divine reality is an extension of the inner-Triadic process of Life and Love, and because it is against the infinite divine wisdom of God to annihilate His beloved creature.

The motive is one, unique, and identical with the inner-Triadic Life and Love. It is eternal and identical with the eternal plan of God concerning His creature, the whole extra-divine reality. It is concerned with the necessary self-love of the Triadic God, the most perfect social and unique being, who loves creatures in Himself and because of Himself, because in Him and for Him they move, and are, and have being and consistency.

Seen in this light, we accept the challenge of Teilhard's incomplete Christology. We keep the very fruitful, penetrating, and valuable elements in his thought, and purifying it of certain confused and anthropomorphic aspects, we can gain a much deeper understanding of all the mysteries of Christianity and their unity in God's plan. For this challenge, the theologian can and must be profoundly thankful. For Teilhard's very valuable contributions to a fuller Christology, we are all in his debt.

celibacy and eastern tradition

Originally published in *Celibacy: The Necessary Option,* edited by George H. Frein
(New York: Herder and Herder, 1968), pp.32-72. Reprinted here with permission.

CELIBACY
AND EASTERN TRADITION

PETRO B. T. BILANIUK

PREFACE

Today for many reasons an attempt to write authoritatively on any of the subjects pertaining to the history or life of Oriental Christianity appears to be an almost insurmountable task. First of all, it seems that we are now only at the very beginning of scholarly research in this area, that is, at the very beginning of the discovery, organization, and critical evaluation of its sources.[1] There is also a very profound change in attitude, approach, and mentality taking place in the Western scholarly world in respect to the Oriental world in general and Oriental Christianity in particular.[2]

In the past, Western theology, philosophy, historiography, and

[1] This is exemplified by such collections of documents as *Monumenta Ucrainae Historica*, Rome, I (1964), II (1965).

[2] The best example of this among the official documents seems to be the *Decree on Eastern Catholic Churches* of Vatican II. Further, there is the publication of the Sacra Congregazione per la Chiesa Orientale, *Oriente Christiano: Cenni storici e statistiche*, Vatican City, 1962. There are many collections and periodicals concerned with the Christian East, among which excels *Orientalia Christiana Analecta* published by the Pontifical Institute of Oriental Studies in Rome. The same change of attitude is also noticeable among the Orthodox theologians in respect to Western Christian theology. J. Meyendorff-N. Afanasieff-R. P. A. Schmemann-N. Koulomzine, *The Primacy of Peter in the Orthodox Church*, London, 1963, represents an achieve-

32

generally all areas of investigation and scholarly research, were arguing from the point of view of strength, conviction of superiority, and a profound, almost blinding persuasion that Western civilization in its material and spiritual aspects, including Western Christianity, is the highest and the most perfect expression of the human achievement, possesses a universal value for the whole of mankind and for all times, and is the only one entitled to establish some authoritative patterns for future development.[3]

Needless to say, Oriental cultures, ancient civilizations, and especially religious systems and Churches were looked upon as exotic museum pieces, antiques, as well as sterile, puerile, or senile goods incapable of enriching and fructifying the future development of mankind and especially of Western Christianity. Fortunately today, because of many factors and an ecumenical spirit, this attitude is changing rapidly, and along with it the very appearance and structure, and partly even the contents, of Western Christianity. Because of political, economical, and social changes Western Christianity reviews its own historical past and is surprised to find in its foundation very definite Oriental Christian forms and ideas, which are able to revive the life of the whole Church of Christ or his divided body.

Some of the Oriental elements rediscovered by Western Christianity, and especially by the Latin Church, are in the liturgy: vernacular languages, concelebration, liturgical litanies, holy communion under two species for the laity in certain circumstances, procession around the altar, etc.[4] In theology, major "orientalizing" elements are: the decision of Pius XII about the

---

ment which was unthinkable in the Orthodox Church just two decades ago. The same must be said of John Meyendorff, *Orthodoxy and Catholicity*, New York, 1966.

[3] Even such excellent work like M. Jugie, *Theologia Dogmatica Christianorum Orientalium*, I–V, Paris, 1926–1935, is not entirely immune to this attitude of superiority.

[4] See *Constitution on the Sacred Liturgy* of Vatican II.

imposition of hands as the matter of the sacrament of orders,[5] as well as the decisions of the Vatican Council II concerning the collegiality of the episcopal body under and with the Pope in ruling the universal Church;[6] the theology of the laity in the Church;[7] the almost purely Oriental theological explanation of the liturgy of the Church,[8] or of the Church in the world which is based on the theology of the Oriental Fathers of the Church;[9] the theology of the local Church and its dignity; and so forth.

Yet one of the most far-reaching and "orientalizing" decisions of Vatican II was an approbation in principle of the married and permanent diaconate.[10] It represents also a tacit admission of a monumental failure on the part of the Roman Catholic Church and its discipline in regard to the major orders and the celibacy attached to them. It further constitutes the first major and practical revision of the existing conception of the hierarchy in the Latin Church, which after some development will culminate in the introduction of an optional celibacy and consequently of the married clergy. In turn, it will create a much closer bond of unity and cooperation between the hierarchy and the laity. From an ecumenical point of view, the introduction of the married and permanent diaconate in the Latin Church is a major victory of all Christian communities and Churches which share one common element, the married clergy, in opposition to the concept and practice of an exclusively celibate hierarchy in the Latin Church, which under this aspect appears to be the most

[5] See Pius XII, Apostolic Constitution "Sacramentum Ordinis," *AAS* 40 (1948), 5–7.

[6] See *Dogmatic Constitution on the Church,* arts. 18–27. The establishment of the Synod of Bishops as an auxiliary body of the Pope is a practical application of the decision on collegiality. See Paul VI, "Apostolica sollicitudo," September 15, 1965.

[7] See *Dogmatic Constitution on the Church,* arts. 30–38, and *Decree on the Apostolate of the Laity* of Vatican II.

[8] See note 4.

[9] See *Pastoral Constitution on the Church in the Modern World* of Vatican II.

[10] See *Dogmatic Constitution on the Church,* art. 29.

34

isolated Church in Christianity. It is the duty of all ecumenically minded Christians to help to extend this victory to the next order of the hierarchy of the Latin Church, or the presbyterate. I am convinced that in the long run all Christian Churches will admit even married bishops as the leaders and centers of Christian unity.

In concluding this introduction I would like to add an autobiographical note. I am a married layman and a member of the Ukrainian Catholic Church. For five years I was the object of seminary education in three different Latin seminaries, which tried to educate me primarily as a celibate, unsuccessfully, I should say, and secondarily as a Latinized Oriental-rite priest, unsuccessfully too. This is so, because after a lengthy period of fighting for my traditional right to become a married priest, I won the battle and received the appropriate permission. Yet, at least for the time being, I have decided to remain a layman. Therefore, my consent to participate in the work of the National Association for Pastoral Renewal and of the present symposium was not motivated by a personal need. Rather, I feel that it is my duty as a Christian and an ecumenically minded theologian to correct defects in Christianity. I am convinced that the absence of the married clergy in the Latin Church is a serious defect and a source of great distress for many thousands of Christians. It is also a very great loss of a tremendous ecclesial potential which is becoming more obvious every day and which we cannot and may not afford to ignore.

I will restrict myself to three main areas:

(1) On the canonical and theological understanding of celibacy and married clergy in the Oriental Churches. A brief excursus on celibacy and married clergy in the Church of Rome until A.D. 386.

(2) The attitude of the Popes and the Holy See in respect to married clergy and celibacy in the Eastern Churches.

(3) Some theological considerations and practical conclusions.

35

I.

ON THE CANONICAL AND THEOLOGICAL UNDERSTANDING OF CELIBACY AND MARRIED CLERGY IN THE ORIENTAL CHURCHES

The absolute majority of Oriental Christians, from the apostles to the present day, understand the witness of the holy Scriptures concerning the married clergy and virginity in the following fashion: Neither our Lord, nor the apostles, nor St. Paul, expressed a command that the ministers of the word and the community of believers in Jesus be unmarried or abstain from the sacrament of marriage or its rightful use.[11] Moreover, all of the apostles, as it seems, with the exceptions of St. John and St. Paul, were married men who in turn imposed their hands upon married men and ordained them to all hierarchical offices in the sub-apostolic Church.[12] Quite independent of the hierarchical offices and the ministry in the Church of the Lord is virginity. It is a special vocation, or a charism of the Holy Spirit, which is primarily something spiritual and secondarily something corporeal. It is a gift given gratuitously to a few primarily for their own sanctification and only secondarily for the edification of the body of Christ. It can and must be proposed to the faithful as an ideal, but it cannot be legislated upon adequately by anybody.[13]

[11] Very useful discussion of the biblical data concerning celibacy, married clergy, and virginity can be found in *Catholicus, Um den Zölibat: Eine Studie und Diskussionsgrundlage*, Zurich, 1966, pp. 17–29.

[12] See E. Schillebeeckx, *Der Amtszölibat: Eine kritische Besinnung*, Düsseldorf, 1967, pp. 15–20.

[13] Many Oriental Fathers and Church writers expressed this spirit: Eusebius, *Demonstr. evang.*, I, 9 (*PG* 22, 81); Cyril of Jerusalem, *Catech.*, XII, 25 (*PG* 33, 757); Nymesius, *Epist.*, 105 (*PG* 66, 1485); Epiphanius, *Adv. haereses*, II, panarion 48, n. 9 (*PG* 41, 867–868), panarion 59, n. 4

All of this is based on a genuine, critical, and unprejudiced understanding of many texts, especially of Matthew 19, 12, 1 Timothy 3, 1f., and 1 Corinthians 7, 25, where St. Paul, himself an unmarried man, says quite emphatically: "Now concerning virgins I have no commandment of the Lord, yet I give an opinion, as one having obtained mercy from the Lord to be trustworthy." The tenor of the remaining chapter is clearly an elaboration on virginity as an evangelical counsel and not a command. Also it is not linked in any way with the hierarchical offices in the Church. Therefore, all attempts to trace and find a proof of celibacy of the clergy in the times of the apostles failed miserably[14] and have been convincingly refuted.[15]

Because they show evidence of a correct understanding of the biblical message, the writings of the early Oriental Fathers of the Church and the canonical legislation of the Eastern Churches concerning married and unmarried clergy are much more biblical, restrained, balanced, and human than those of the Western Church; and they are also free of many preconceived ideas borrowed from pagan philosophies and heretical Christian aberrations. Eastern Christianity, due to its geographical position, was subjected to many and much stronger pressures from different Oriental religions and philosophical and cultural trends than Western Christianity. Among them, Gnosticism, Manicheism, and the exaggerated spiritualism of Neoplatonism are the most

---

(PG 41, 1021–1025); *Expositio fidei*, 21 (PG 42, 823–826); Eusebius of Caesarea, *Demonstratio evang.*, I, 9; Methodius, *Symposion*, Oratio III, 13 (PG 18, 82); Synesius, *Epist.*, 105 (PG 66, 1485).

[14] Especially famous in this respect is M. G. Bickell, "Der Cölibat, eine apostolische Anordnung," *Zeitschrift für katholische Theologie*, 2 (1878), 26–64; 3 (1879) 792–799.

[15] A definitive refutation of Bickell's thesis was given by F.-X. Funk, *Tübinger theologische Quartalschrift*, 61 (1897) 205–247; "Cölibat und Priesterehe im christlichen Altertum," *Kirchengeschichtliche Abhandlungen und Untersuchungen*, Paderborn, 1897, pp. 121–155, and E. Vacandarol, "Les Origines du célibat ecclésiastique," *Études de critique et d'histoire religieuse*, Paris, 1913, pp. 69–120; "Célibat ecclésiastique," *DTC* (Paris, 1932), II, 2068–2078.

prominent. A great help to Oriental Christianity in finding and maintaining this balance concerning married clergy, celibacy, and virginity was a positive theological approach to created reality in general, and to matter, marriage, and sexuality in particular.[16] It was anchored in the Scriptures and reflected in the spiritual optimism of the early Oriental Fathers of the Church and the magnificent Oriental liturgies.[17] This spiritual optimism was founded upon a firm conviction that created reality is good, that it is being redeemed, transfigured, sanctified, and fulfilled by the Triadic God, that is, by God the Father, through the Son, and in the Holy Spirit.[18] Yet, despite its evident superiority over the legislation of the Western Christianity, the legislation of Eastern Christianity concerning celibacy and married clergy exhibits also some theological and practical imperfections, which we will try to portray during our presentation.

The history of the canonical and theological understanding of celibacy and married clergy in the Oriental Churches can be resumed as follows: the Apostolic Church Ritual (written *c.* 300 in Egypt) sums up very well the patristic tradition of the first three centuries of Christianity concerning the marital status of the clergy when it says that the unmarried state of the bishops and priests is "seemly" "fitting."[19] This means that the unmarried or virginal state of a clergyman was strongly recommended. The first synodal decisions came about at the beginning of the fourth century, because in 314 two regional synods took place which

---

[16] On these matters see M. J. Le Guillou, O.P., *The Spirit of Eastern Orthodoxy*, Glen Rock, New Jersey, 1964; Julius Tyciak, *Zwischen Morgenland und Abendland*, Düsseldorf, 1949; Paul Evdokimov, *Die Frau und das Heil der Welt*, Munich, 1960.

[17] Among them the *Liturgy of St. Basil the Great*, and especially the *Anaphora*, occupy the most prominent place.

[18] One of many beautiful examples of this are the writings of St. Athanasius of Alexandria. See Pius Merendino, O.S.B., *Osterbriefe des Apa Athanasios*, Düsseldorf, 1965; also B. Altaner, *Patrologie*, Freiburg, 1958, pp. 214–241.

[19] See Michael Pfliegler, *Celibacy*, London, p. 24.

38

dealt with the marriage of the clergy. The first was the Council of Ancyra, which decreed that clergy in major orders may not enter into marriage. Yet it made an exception of an unmarried deacon, who at the time of ordination reserved himself the right to future marriage. An unmarried deacon, who did not make this type of reservation, would lose his office if he should marry.[20] The second council was celebrated at Neocaesarea. In canon 1 it threatened with deposition a priest who marries.[21]

It is important to note that these decisions came about one year after the Edict of Milan of 313, when the Church as a legal institution in the Roman Empire was acquiring wealth, prestige, and related economic, political, and social problems. Therefore, the Church became much more aware of, and started to understand as a strict command, Paul's counsel to deacons, presbyters, and bishops to be "married but once," which is contained in 1 Timothy 3, 12 and Titus 1f. Thus, primarily for economic and social reasons, the Church began a much stricter enforcement of the tradition prohibiting ordination of all digamous candidates, and the celebration of a first or a second marriage after the ordination.

During the first ecumenical council of Nikaia (325), some bishops, inspired by the famous decisions of the puritanical synod of Elvira in Spain (about 300 or 306), wanted to impose a perfect marital continence upon all bishops, presbyters, and deacons in the Church universal. How this motion was defeated is reported to us by the Greek historian Socrates in his famous *Historia ecclesiastica,* book I, Chapter XI. I quote my own literal translation of this important witness:

[20] Canon 10, Mansi II, 517. Later on the Council of Gangres recognized the same right to priests. It also cast an anathema on all those who pretended that it is indecent or unseemly to participate in the celebration of the mysteries with a married priest: see canon 4, Mansi II, 1101.

[21] See E. Herman, "Célibat des Clercs: En droit oriental," *Dictionnaire de droit canonique,* III, Paris, 1942, 147.

39

But because we promised above that we shall make mention of Paphnutios and Spyridonos, it is fitting here to speak a little about them. Paphnutios indeed was a bishop of a city in upper Thebes: he was a pious man and dear to God, because wonderous signs were performed by him. In the time of persecution he had lost his eye. Indeed, the Emperor respected (this) man very much, and called him frequently to (his) palace and kissed his torn-out eye. Such was Emperor Constantine's reverence (towards him). And this should be said by us about Paphnutios in the first place. Now we shall report of what indeed has been done by his counsel for the benefit of the Church and the order of the clergy. It occurred to the bishops to introduce a new law in the Church, that all clergymen, I mean the bishops, and the presbyters, and the deacons, abstain from intercourse with (their) spouse, whom they had married while being laymen. And when the question was asked about this of everyone present, Paphnutios, rising up in the middle of the gathering of bishops, protested vehemently that this heavy yoke should not be placed upon the clergy: (for) marriage is honorable and intercourse is pure, he said, (and) out of an excessive severity injury should not be inflicted on the Church, because not all are able to follow the discipline of such a strict continence, and possibly from that it could happen that the chastity of the wife of each of them would not be preserved. (Also) he called the coming together of a husband and of a legitimate wife chastity. It is sufficient that, according to an ancient tradition of the Church, those who were inscribed into the clergy marry no more; but it is not possible to separate anybody from her, whom he legitimately had married before, when he was a layman. And he said this being himself not only fully inexperienced in marriage, but also in intercourse with a woman; indeed, since his boyhood he was educated in a monastery and was praised by all for his exceptional chastity. For the rest, the whole assembly of priests assented to the speech of Paphnutios. Hence, terminating the discussion of this matter, they left it to the discretion of each of them, that they abstain from the intercourse with (their) spouses, if they want to. And this is indeed (the story) of Paphnutios.[22]

Needless to say, the authenticity and historicity of this account of Bishop Paphnutios by the historian Socrates was denied by

[22] *PG* 67, 101–104; the same story with some additions is repeated by Sozomenos, *Hist. Eccl.* I, 23 (*PG* 67, 925).

many Latins, who in their apologies of abolute clerical celibacy approached the whole complex of questions with a definitely preconceived set of notions.[23] There were even attempts to disprove the above account by a reinterpretation of the third canon of the same Council of Nikaia which reads: "The Great Synod has strictly forbidden to bishop, priest, and deacon, and to every ecclesiastic, to have a 'subintroduced woman,' except perhaps a mother, a sister, an aunt, or such person only as may be above suspicion."[24] However, it is clear that this canon is directed against those members of the clergy who used to play the role of celibates, but kept *agapetae* or concubines in their households.[25]

The story of Paphnutios is remarkable, because it witnesses to many important moments during the first and probably the most important ecumenical council of Nikaia. First of all, it strengthened prohibition of marriage in orders and the ordination of digami, but they decided not to prohibit married men to orders and rejected compulsory separation from their wives of those who had been married previously to ordination. Also, the Fathers of the Council of Nikaia were convinced of the sanctity and chastity of marriage and of the marital act. They were also conscious of the dignity of the human person and felt themselves competent to legislate on the most solemn profession of our

[23] For example, *Valesii Annotationes* to this text in *PG* 67, 101–102 "Cæterum tota hæc narratio de Paphnutio et de cælibatu clericorum, prorsus suspecta mihi videtur. Nam nec Rufinus, ex quo priora de Paphnutio hausit Socrates, ullam hujus rei mentionem facit: nec Paphnutius ullus memoratus inter episcopos Aegypti qui Nicæno concilio interfuerunt. De cælibatu autem episcoporum, presbyterorum ac diaconorum, exstat decretum Siricii PP., cap. 7; item Innocentii PP., cap. 16; item Leonis PP., cap. 17." A very apt refutation of these objections are given by Henry C. Lea, *History of Sacerdotal Celibacy in the Christian Church*, I, London, 1907, pp. 45–54. Both Theodoret, *Hist. Eccl.* I, 7, and Rufinus, *Hist. Eccl.*, X, 4, claim that Paphnutios was present at the Council of Nicæa in 325.

[24] For the Greek original and Latin translation see *Conciliorum Oecumenicorum Decreta*, Basel, 1962, 6. (Abbreviation used: *COD.*)

[25] See H. C. Lea, *History of Sacredotal Celibacy in the Christian Church*, I, London, 1907, pp. 45–54.

faith; yet they considered themselves incapable of legislating in an area which must be left to the personal decision of each member of the clergy, especially concerning the use or non-use of one's marriage rights. They did not forget the dignity of the wives of the clergy either.

Moreover, the Fathers of the Council of Nikaia were afraid of latent encratic tendencies and therefore did not hesitate in the very first canon to condemn, bar from ordination and promotion, and depose all those who like Origen and some of his followers dared to castrate themselves.[26] All this proves that they still were very much aware of the sanctity and divinization with transfiguration of the whole created extra-divine reality on account of its very creation by the Triadic God, the redemption and sanctification by the incarnate Logos, and the present and future eschatological fulfillment by the Triadic God.[27]

The same awareness was still very strong in the East during the celebration of the Roman Synod of 386[28] under the presidency of Pope Siricius, which approved the puritanical decisions of the Council of Elvira.[29] This is so because the sixth of the 85 "Apostolic Canons" (= 47th chapter of the "Apostolic Constitutions" written c. 380 in Syria) actually forbids bishops, priests, and deacons under pain of deposition to leave their wives on the false pretext of piety or chastity.[30] Thus the protection of the marriage rights of a woman married to a clergyman became reality, and she ceased to be considered an impersonal entity or a property of her clergyman-husband. The imperial decree of the

[26] See *COD* 5.

[27] This doctrine was still very much alive in the writings of Cyril of Alexandria, for example, *Thesaurus de SS. Trinitate*, assert 15 (*PG* 75, 292–293).

[28] See P. Jaffé, *Regesta pontificum romanorum ab condita ecclesia ad annum post Christum natum 1198*, I, Leipzig, 1881, 41; see also Pope Siricius, *Epist. ad Himerium Tarrac.* (PL 56, 558–559, 562).

[29] See Mansi II, 11; English texts of canons 18, 27, and 33 in Pfliegler, *op. cit.*, pp. 25–26.

[30] See Mansi I, 51, and *PG* 1, 957.

42

emperors Honorius and Theodosius in 420 confirmed the "Apostolic Canons" and "Apostolic Constitutions" in this area and prohibited the clergy of all the orders to separate themselves from their wives under the pretext of chastity or piety.[31] The same decision entered into the definitive legislation of the Trullanum II of 692 and is binding as a law up to the present day.[32]

Here again there is a superiority of the Eastern tradition over the Western, for some Western prelates, synods, and canonists during certain periods of Western Christianity and in certain places had no scruples about selling the wives and children of their clergymen of major orders into slavery and appropriate the money thus obtained for a noble cause of the extension of God's kingdom on earth.[33]

It was only natural that with the strengthening of the monastic tradition in the East (since the fourth century), more and more bishops were chosen from among the outstanding monastic personalities, that is, those who from the Holy Spirit received a charism of virginity and were recognized as such by the Church and "tonsured into the monkhood" (in opposition to the West-

[31] *Codex Theodos.*, 1, xvi, tit. 2, lex. 44.

[32] See canons 6, 12, 13, and 48: Mansi XI, 944–948 and 965. See also *Decretum Gratiani*, d. 31, c. 13 and 14.

[33] Pfliegler, *op. cit.*, pp. 30–31, writes: "The Synod of Pavia (1081) went even further as regards the carrying out of these decrees and declared in shrill tones which offend our sensibilities more today than they did then, that children of priests were slaves of the Church! The German Pope, St. Leo IX, extended this dictate to include priests' wives (1049)." *Ibid.*, pp. 35–36: "The Synod of Melfi, 1081 [southern Italy] gave the princes power [in canons 9, 12, 14] to make slaves of the clergy's women and wives. Their sons were declared bastard, but allowed the right to enter a monastery or canonry. A new canon appeared which declared all those who attended mass celebrated by a priest who kept concubines to be excommunicated. The unpleasant consequences of this, such as witch hunts for priest women, were repugnant even to those who supported the reform."

Writing of the introduction of celibacy in medieval Hungary, Pfliegler says on p. 38: "The Synod of Szaboles [end of the eleventh century] set down marriage for priests as something naturally taken for granted. It decreed: . . . 2. Any priest who lives with a girl as though he were married to her must deliver her up to be sold [as a slave]. The money from this transaction is to go to the bishopric!"

ern conception of a religious profession).[34] Therefore, in their case we cannot speak of celibacy as it is being understood in the West today. It seems that towards the end of the fourth century, when a married man was chosen to become a bishop, he had two alternatives: the first was to send his wife, with her consent, of course, to a distant monastery, and this was the preferable alternative; the second was to accept his nomination to the bishopric with a reservation of his right to keep his wife after the episcopal consecration and during the exercise of his episcopal ministry.[35]

In the fourth and fifth centuries, therefore, there were no strict laws in the Eastern Churches concerning celibacy and married clergy, and the accepted traditions were very diversified. It seems that in most of the Eastern countries the married bishops were still in existence in great numbers. In Egypt most of the bishops were unmarried. In Thessaly, Macedonia, and Greece, married members of major orders kept their wives, whom they had married before their ordination, but were expected to live with them like brothers with sisters, which is a polite way of saying that they had to abstain from sexual intercourse. If they did not comply they were expected to be deposed. Nobody, however, was able to enforce strictly these traditions, and to the generally accepted rules there were always many exceptions.[36]

The first canonical decision concerning the married and unmarried bishops was not a work of ecclesiastical legislator, but an evil growing out of Byzantine caesaropapism. It was Basileios Justinianos who in 528 issued a decree making it a law that

[34] On monasticism in Eastern Christianity see Ernst Benz, *Geist und Leben der Ostkirche*, Hamburg, 1957, pp. 75–88.

[35] Famous is the case of Synesius, a recognized poet and philosopher, who after his election to the bishopric of his home town Ptolemaïs, reserved for himself the right to continue his marriage after his consecration; see *Epist.*, 105 (*PG* 66, 1485).

[36] See Socrates, *Hist. eccl.*, VI, c. 22 (*PG* 67, 637).

44

from the episcopal dignity are excluded all those who had children or grandchildren.[37] Thus married men as yet were not excluded from the episcopal dignity provided that they were childless. However, it implied a very marked preference for unmarried and childless candidates. The reason given for this legislation is a noble one: the engrossing duties of the office, which require that the whole mind and soul should be devoted to them. The secondary reason given is by far more important: it is indecent to convert to the use of the prelate's family the wealth bestowed by the faithful on the Church for pious uses and for charity. However, the real reason remained without any formal enunciation: it was a fear of dissipation of the churchly goods as a result of inheritance by the children of the bishop.

It is almost certain that this law was not strictly observed, for in 535 the Emperor was forced in his *Novellae* to issue a new law repeating the former injunction and adding a restriction on conjugal intercourse of the bishops with their wives. Thus this new law presupposes that the bishop is either unmarried or separated from his wife, or at least that he abstains from his marriage rights. Besides, the emperor decreed that no inquiry be made into previously incurring infractions of the law, but that it be rigidly enforced for the future.[38] This decision regarding the separation of the bishop from his wife was again alluded to in 548, and the same law is carried through the famous *Basilicon* by Leo the Philosopher and the *Nomocanon* of Photius.[39]

In his legislative power, Emperor Justinian did not forget deacons and presbyters either. In 513 he issued a constitution in which he calls attention to the regulation prohibiting the mar-

---

[37] See *Codex Justin.*, constit. xlii, 1. On the legislation of Justinian see Lea, *op. cit.*, I, pp. 92–95.

[38] See *Novellae*, VI, c. 1, §7.

[39] See *Novellae*, CXIII, c. 1; *Novellae*, CXXXVII, c. 2; *Basilicon*, III, 1, c. 8.; *Balsamon Schol. ad Nomocan.*, tit. 1, c. 23.

riage of deacons and subdeacons.[40] In view of the fact that little respect was paid to it, the emperor declared that the children of such unions were spurious and incompetent to inherit anything. Their wives likewise were excluded from inheritence and the whole estate of the uncanonically married subdeacon, or deacon, was given to the Church. In 535 Justinian laid down new regulations in greater detail:[41] anyone who kept an *agapetae* or who has married a divorced woman or a second time was to be held ineligible to the diaconate or priesthood. All subdeacons, deacons, priests, and bishops who took a wife or a concubine either publicly or secretly were to be deposed and lose all clerical privileges. Also, preference was to be given to married clergy who lived in strict continence, but the continuation of the previous marital relations were not subject to any legislative interference. In 545 there was an urgent need to promulgate once more the same laws with an addition that an unmarried postulant for the diaconate must promise that he would not marry, and any bishop permitting such marriage was threatened with degradation.[42] Of course, all of these laws were not strictly adhered to because of the resistance of a great number of clergy to interference by the imperial authorities in the affairs of the Church. What were the reasons why Justinian issued such laws? The traditional privilege of immunity of the clergy which liberated it from all political offices, military service, and taxation had made the clerical office very attractive to many unworthy candidates, and the demand to adhere to the above restrictions was an attempt at keeping away from holy orders all undesirable elements..

The final and official position adopted by Eastern Christianity in respect to married clergy and celibacy was expressed by the decisions of the Council held at Constantinople in 692, which is

[40] See *Codex Justin.*, constit. xlv, cod. I, 3.
[41] See *Novellae*, VI, c. 5; these provisions were repeated the following year (536) in *Novellae*, XXII, c. 42.
[42] See *Novellae*, CXXIII, c. 12 and 14. See *Basilicon*, III, 1, 26; *Balsamon Schol. ad Nomocan.*, tit. 1, c. 23.

46

called *Quinisext in Trullo,* or simply the Second Trullan Synod.[43] The Greeks maintain that this was an ecumenical council and that its legislation is binding upon the whole of Christendom. The Latins claim that it was a provincial and a schismatic council. This council decreed that if a married priest is consecrated a bishop, the marriage has to be ended in mutual consent and the wife has to enter a distant monastery.[44] On the other hand, the priests, the deacons, and the subdeacons may continue a marriage entered into before ordination, but have to practice continence from marital intercourse on the days of holy service. In view of the beginnings of the adverse Latin practices both in the East and West, the Council in Trullo decreed that whoever attempted to separate priests, deacons, or subdeacons from their legitimate wives, would be deposed. Also, a priest, a deacon, or a subdeacon who dismissed his wife under the pretext of piety would be suspended in his office, and, if he persisted in his stance, he was to be deposed.[45] A marriage entered into after ordination to the subdiaconate has to be dissolved, or the clergyman in question is deposed.[46] This, however, does not decide anything concerning the existence of a separating hindrance of marriage. These regulations remained in force in the Eastern Churches to the present day, and were generally recognized by Rome as binding the whole of Oriental Christianity, that is, both the Orthodox Churches and the Catholic Oriental Churches in communion with Rome.[47]

[43] On this council see F. X. Murphy, "Quinisext Synod," *New Catholic Encyclopedia,* XII, New York, 1967, 30. (Abbreviation used: *NCE.*) See also Lea, *op. cit.,* I, pp. 94–98; Vitalien Laurent, "L'Oeuvre canonique du Concile en Trullo (691–692). Source primaire du droit de l'Eglise orientale," *Rev. Et. Byz.,* XXIII (1965), 7–41.

[44] See canon 48, Mansi XI, 965.

[45] See canon 13, Mansi XI, 948.

[46] See canons 3 and 6, Mansi XI, 944.

[47] Thus the apostolic letter "Cleri sanctitati" of Pope Pius XII, June 11, 1957, which contains one part of general Church law for Eastern Catholic Churches (that is, *De ritibus orientalibus* and *De personis*), adheres in general to the decisions of Trullanum II.

However, since these laws were sometimes too harsh and unjust, Eastern Christianity established a tradition of exceptional dispensations. For instance, what to do if the wife of the man married before ordination dies? Should he be punished by this circumstance and lead a celibate life to which he was not called? General practice and common sense found a solution to this problem. If a priest or a deacon after the death of his wife wishes to marry again he must relinquish his office and can be given some lower office in the Church, or be placed as a helper of the bishop in a chancery.[48] Some Eastern Catholic Churches also adhere to this custom. Some under the influence of the Latin legislation remain rigid in their interpretation of the law and do not admit any exception.[49]

But not only this case constituted an exception to this general rule, because some of the Eastern Churches in the course of time adopted a much broader and generous attitude towards the married clergy and especially towards the married bishops. Several major exceptions are known.

The first relaxation of the laws came about in the Nestorian Church with Barsuma, the Nestorian Metropolitan of Nisibis, who c. 480 married a nun.[50] In order to justify his crime he assembled a synod in which the privilege of marriage was granted to all ranks of the clergy and members of the religious state from a tonsured monk to the patriarch himself. However, some fifty-five years later, after many different vicissitudes, the Nestorian Patriarch Mar Aba subjected the bishops of his Church to the decisions of the Greek and Latin Churches. The Nestorian Church is also the best proof that matrimony of the clergy is not incompatible with the ministry and the missionary work. The Nestorians were the only Christians in antiquity and the Middle Ages who extended their missionary work to India, Mon-

[48] See Pfliegler, *op. cit.*, pp. 28–29.
[49] For example, Ukrainians and Ruthenians follow rigorous interpretation of the law prohibiting remarriage of priests.
[50] On this see Lea, *op. cit.*, pp. 98–99; Benz, *op. cit.*, pp. 109–110.

48

golia, and China. Their descendants are to be found to the present day on the coast of Malabar.

Another example are the Monophysites or Copts of Egypt and Ethiopia, who permitted their bishops to retain their wives after the episcopal consecration. However, the second marriage or a marriage in major orders is prohibited, except under dispensation from the Patriarch.[51]

The third exception was a married clergy of the Ukrainian Orthodox Autocephalous Church in the twentieth century, which permitted its bishops to keep their wives after the episcopal consecration, and permitted second and third marriages of the clergy in major orders.[52]

In conclusion it is necessary to point out that Eastern Christianity was rather mild in imposing ecclesiastical penalties of suspension or deposition on those who were breaking the existing laws on married clergy and celibacy. The Western Church went much farther, because a clergyman in higher orders who attempts to contract a marriage is *ipso facto* irregular (*CIC,* canon 985, n. 3), he loses his Church office (c. 188, n. 5), he is excommunicated (c. 2388), and the children of such unions are declared illegitimate (c. 1114). In the Orthodox Eastern Churches any member of the clergy can receive a dispensation to return to the laical state, to marry, to lead a good Christian life, and to rear legitimate children.

An Excursus on Celibacy and Married Clergy in the Church of Rome until A.D. 386

In the first three centuries of Christianity the Church of Rome belonged, practically speaking, to the Greek Church, or at least

[51] See Lea, *op. cit.,* pp. 99–100; also the description of Ethopia by Osorius in Reynaldi, a. 1514, n. 107.

[52] See Mytropolyt Vasyl Lypkivsjkyj, *Vidrodzennja Cerkvy v Ukrajini, 1917–1930,* Toronto, 1959, *passim,* esp. p. 93. The "Kievan Canons" of 1921 of the Ukrainian Autocephalous Orthodox Church permitted married bishops; see p. 60.

was very closely linked to Eastern Christianity. This was so because until the second half of the fourth century (*c.* 360 to 382) the Roman liturgy was celebrated in Greek[53] (the remnants of which are still in use in the Papal Mass), the majority of the Roman Christian community was using Greek as their mother tongue, and generally the cultural and theological ties with the Greek Church were very strong. This was so in contrast to North Africa, Spain, many portions of Italy, and so forth, where the dominant language in the ecclesial life was Latin, and where the cultural, ecclesial, and theological development was taking a much more independent course.

As long as the Church of Rome was closely linked to the Eastern Churches, everything was in perfect order concerning their ideas and practice in the realm of the marital status of the clergy, and there was no mention of celibacy, but of virginity only. Many members of the ministering hierarchy were married, including some forty Popes, of whom many continued their marriage in their office as the Bishop of Rome.[54] Needless to say, nobody was scandalized, because this was considered to be a personal area and within the realm of conscience of each of the clergymen.

The trouble started after the dying out of the Greek language in Rome and a gradual decline of the close ties with Eastern Christianity, because a very marked "Westernization" of the Roman Christian Community took place, that is, a gradual increase of influences from the provinces, and in the case of celibacy from Spain. Thus a Synod of Rome in 386[55] under Pope Siricius accepted the harsh and puritanical decisions concern-

---

[53] See C. R. A. Cunliffe, "Liturgical Languages," *NCE*, VIII, 898. It was probably Pope Damasus I (366–384) who introduced Latin as the liturgical language in Rome.

[54] See Philipp Hiltebrandt, *Papsttum und Kirche: Epochen der Papstgeschichte, Aufbau und Organisation der Weltkirche*, Stuttgart, 1957, p. 171; Prinz Z. V. Lobkowitz, *Statistik der Päpste*, Freiburg, 1905.

[55] For references see note 28.

50

ing married clergy promulgated by the regional Synod of Elvira, which took place in A.D. 300 or 306.

Let us quote the three pertinent canons of the Synod of Elvira:[56]

Canon 18. "Bishops, priests, and deacons who are found guilty of incontinence during their period of service, are not even to be allowed to receive communion before death, because of the scandal of such a palpable offense."

Canon 27. "The bishop and the priest in general may have in his household only his sister, or his daughter, and only then if they are virgins and are betrothed to God."

Canon 33. "Bishops, priests, and deacons, and all clergy in general who have altar service to perform, must refrain from intercourse with their wives, and are not allowed to beget children. If they oppose this, they forfeit their official position."

It is important to add that Pope Siricius and the Roman Synod of 386, by accepting the decisions of the Synod of Elvira, disregarded the spirit and some of the decisions of the first ecumenical council of Nikaia of 325, where the motion to accept the decisions of the Council of Elvira which was proposed by Western Fathers of the Council was defeated on account of the intervention of Bishop Paphnutios. They also disregarded the authority of the "Apostolic Constitutions" and the "Apostolic Canons," all of which repudiated the harshness and puritanism of the decisions of the Council of Elvira. Besides, Pope Siricius in a letter to Himerius[57] expressed the intention to extend the above-mentioned legislation to the whole of the Latin Church. Therefore, the alienation between Eastern and Western Christianity did not start as a result of the revolt of Photius and Cerularius in the ninth and the eleventh centuries respectively, but already in the fourth century as a result of a major departure of the Roman Church from the sub-apostolic tradition in respect

[56] Quoted by Pfliegler, *op. cit.*, pp. 25–26.
[57] *PL* 56, 558–559, 562.

to the married clergy. However, the practical enforcement of the absolute celibacy of the clergy which started with the Councils of Elvira and Rome (386) took more than a millennium.[58]

II.

THE ATTITUDE OF THE POPES AND THE HOLY SEE IN RESPECT TO MARRIED CLERGY AND CELIBACY IN THE EASTERN CHURCHES

Without a doubt the most far-reaching aspect of the encyclical *Sacerdotalis Caelibatus* of Pope Paul VI is its very positive approach to the tradition of Eastern Christianity concerning celibacy and married clergy. For example, paragraph 38 of this encyclical reads: "If the legislation of the Eastern Church is different in the matter of discipline with regard to clerical celibacy, as was finally established by the Council in Trullo held in the year 692, and which has been clearly recognized by the Second Vatican Council, this is due to the different historical background of that most noble part of the Church, a situation which the Holy Spirit has providentially and supernaturally influenced.

"We ourselves take this opportunity to express our esteem and our respect for all the clergy of the Oriental Churches, and to recognize in them examples of fidelity and zeal which make them worthy of sincere veneration."[59]

However, paragraph 40 of the same document does not fail to make the following observation: "Further, it is by no means

[58] It was only the institution of the seminaries for the future clerics by the Council of Trent (Sessio XXIII, Decreta super reformatione, canon 18: *COD* 726, 25–729, 23) which definitely finished the tradition of clandestine marriages of the clergy which were invalid.

[59] This encyclical was published on June 24, 1967. We quote the English text as it appeared in print in *St. Louis Review,* June 30, 1967.

52

futile to observe that in the East only celibate priests are ordained bishops, and priests themselves cannot contract marriage after their ordination to the priesthood. This indicates that these venerable Churches also possess to a certain extent the principle of a celibate priesthood. It shows too that there is a certain appropriateness for the Christian priesthood, of which the bishops possess the summit and the fullness, of the observance of celibacy."

In order to appreciate adequately these statements, it is worthwhile to examine briefly the history of the ever changing attitudes of the Popes and the Roman See in respect to the married clergy and celibacy in the Eastern Churches.[60]

Evidently, as long as the Latin Church was still in the difficult process of introducing absolute clerical celibacy in the West, it had little time or power to turn its attention to the Eastern Churches in this delicate matter. Therefore, the Popes and the Roman Curia looked upon the married clergy of the East as a self-evident reality about which little could be done or said. Thus, for example, Pope Innocent III (1198–1216), in a letter dated September 5, 1203, recognized the fact that the Oriental Church does not impose the vow of continence on its clergy and that Oriental clergymen can marry as long as they are in their minor orders.[61] The same is true of Innocent IV (1243–1245), who in his bull "Sub catholicae professione fidei" decreed that married Oriental priests may hear confessions.[62] In this period of time the Popes were still very generous in this respect not

[60] In the presentation of this section of the paper (that is, history from 1203 to the end of the nineteenth century), we rely mainly on the excellent presentation by Wilhelm de Vries, *Rom und die Patriarchate des Ostens*, Munich, 1963, pp. 237–241. See also *Codificazione Canonica Orientale*, Fonti, Series I, Vatican City, 1930; Fonti, Series II, Vatican City, 1935; Fonti, Series III, Vatican City, 1943. (Abbreviation used: Fontes Series.) See *Bullarium Romanus* (Taurinii, 1957–1872), I–XXIII.

[61] See Fontes Series III, vol. II, 240–241, no. 40, letter dated September 5, 1203.

[62] See *Bullarium Romanum* III, 582, §13.

only in some distant Oriental lands, but also close to their own home; thus in 1284 Pope Martin IV condemned an apparently widespread abuse in Sicily, where clergymen born out of Latin-rite parents used to contract a marriage before the reception of the major orders and continue it after ordination. However, for the sons born out of the Greek-rite parents he let this pass as a matter of course.[63]

The most generous and most far-reaching attitude was that of Pope Clement V, who in 1307 gave to missionaries working in the Orient an extraordinary authority to allow Oriental clergy-men who had married after receiving major orders to continue their marriages.[64] This case is very interesting for our contemporary situation, and the commentary to it can be resumed in a brief sentence: If Clement V in the Oriental Church, why not Paul VI in the Latin Church?

Subsequent years saw the first negative attitude of Rome and a first major clash with an Eastern Church in these questions. It was during the pontificate of Pope Benedict XII in 1375 that in Rome a long report "On the Errors of the Armenians" was elaborated. In this report the Armenians are accused of allowing their deacons to marry with the permission of their bishops and still raise them to the priesthood.[65] The marriage, therefore, of the lower clergy was considered legitimate by the Roman canonists. This reproach has been rejected as unfounded by the Synod of the Armenian Church which was celebrated in Sis in 1345.[66] It is relatively easy to see why at this time the Latins started to be scandalized by the Oriental practices regarding married clergy: the decisions of the First (1123)[67] and the Second Lateran Council (1139)[68] on the nullity and validity of mar-

63 See Fontes Series III, vol. V/2, 115, no. 240.
64 See *ibid.*, vol. VII/1, 26, no. 74.
65 See *ibid.*, vol. VIII, 150, no. 391, XCIII.
66 See *ibid.*, vol. VIII, 222, no. 596.
67 See Mansi XXI, 286.
68 See *ibid.*, 715 (*COD* 174, 1–16). The decisive sentence was: "Huius-modi namque copulationem, quam contra ecclesiasticam regulam constat esse contractam, matrimonium non esse censemus."

riages attempted by clergymen in major orders started really to take effect and were confirmed and expounded in greater detail by many local synods, especially of Bremen in 1266[69] and Valladolid in 1322.[70]

One of the cornerstones of the Council of Florence (1439) was the preservation of the customs and rites of the Greeks and other Orientals, and of the rights and privileges of the Eastern Patriarchs.[71] This means also a preservation of the Oriental Church discipline concerning married clergy and celibacy and the right of the Oriental patriarchs to regulate and legislate in this area. In this spirit, Pope Gregory XIII recognized the fact of the married clergy in the Maronite Church and made reference to Pope Stephen, who let stand the old tradition of the Orientals in this point.[72]

Under Pope Urban VIII (1623–1644) the question of celibacy of the Orientals became again very acute. It was occasioned by a report of the missionaries in the East that some of the priests of the Chaldean rite married after their ordination to the presbyterate. The whole question was dealt with by the Sacred Congregation for the Propagation of the Faith. A lengthy and

[69] Pfliegler, op. cit., p. 37 writes: "The Synod of Bremen (1266) took stern measures against this disregard of the law [that is, of celibacy imposed by Lateran II]:

1. Bishops who give dispensation from the ban on marriage are excommunicated.

2. All those who give their daughter in marriage to priests are also excommunicated.

3. Children resulting from a priest's marriage may not inherit.

4. Priests who keep concubines forfeit the benefice."

[70] This council denied concubines the right to a Church burial.

[71] The Council of Florence in its fourth session (July 6, 1439) published its definition, "Laetentur caeli et exultet terra," which was an act of reunion of the Roman and the Oriental Church. For the Greek Fathers of the Council the decisive passage reads: 'Moreover we renew the order of the venerable patriarchs, which was handed down in the sacred canons, [and decide] that the patriarch of Constantinople be the second after the most holy Roman pontiff, the third indeed of Alexandria, the fourth moreover of Antiochia, and the fifth of Jerusalem, evidently without [any] infraction of all their privileges and right" (COD 504).

[72] See R. De Martinis, Iuris Pontificii de Propaganda Fide, III, Rome, 1888–1909, 227, §34.

complex discussion issued which focused upon the central question, whether the celibacy rule was of divine or human origin. There was no agreement, but the latter solution seemed preferable. Therefore, a meeting of the Propaganda which was held on September 18, 1629, decided that if celibacy should be of human origin, then the Pope could dispense, because of the human weakness of the Chaldean priests in question.[73] Apparently, nobody was aware of the generous decision of Clement V issued 322 years earlier, and the subsequent decisions of Rome were progressively stiffer and stiffer. Thus on August 3, 1650, the Holy Office decided that the marriages of the Nestorian priests, which they had contracted after their ordination to the major orders, could not be recognized and that dispensations cannot be given, because the Holy Apostolic See did not grant such dispensations.[74] In 1660 the Holy Office decided once more against the validity of marriages of priests, but this time recommended the granting of dispensation in the cases under consideration.[75] All decisions taken by the Roman Curia in this area were made according to the Church law of the Byzantine Church in a narrow Latin interpretation. The Curia seems to have been ignorant of the Nestorian tradition, which was much more broad-minded in this point than the Greek tradition.[76]

An indiscriminate application of the Byzantine legislation on celibacy and married clergy to all Orientals is very vividly illustrated in the case of Pope Benedict XIV (1740–1758). In his apostolic instruction *Eo quamvis tempore* dated May 4, 1745, he recognized explicitly the Oriental legislation on this point, but without hesitation he applied the Greek legislation to the Copts and declared that Oriental clergymen can contract a mar-

[73] See *ibid.*, II, 43, no. LXXI.
[74] See *ibid.*, II, 107, no. CCV.
[75] See *ibid.*, II, 118, no. CCXXX.
[76] See J. Dauvillier-C. De Clercq, *Le Mariage en droit canonique oriental*, Paris, 1936, p. 174; J. B. Chabot, *Synodicon Orientale ou recueil des synodes nestoriens*, Paris, 1902, pp. 303–305.

56

riage before but not after receiving the order of diaconate.[77] He did not know that the Coptic tradition allowed the marriage of the deacons, but not of the priests.[78] Benedict XII dealt again with the question of celibacy in his constitution *Allatae sunt* dated April 26, 1775. Here again he stressed that a married clergy in the Eastern Churches is a legitimate thing in accordance with the Oriental Church law. The Holy See does not abolish it in order not to frighten the Greeks away from the union. The Greek tradition, he declared, contradicts neither the positive divine law nor the natural law. In a polemical tone he added that the Greeks may not accuse the Latins of being despisers of marriage on account of the celibacy of their clergy.[79]

For practical reasons Benedict XII in his constitution *Etsi pastoralis* dated July 1, 1774, permitted a married clergy to the Italo-Greeks living in Latin surroundings. Yet, he did not fail to express his wish that Greek priests would also live up to the ideal of celibacy.[80] Benedict XII represents a period of transition from recognition to toleration, and from toleration to mounting pressures against the married clergy in the Eastern Churches. The Roman Curia was gradually losing an inner respect for the Oriental customs in general and of married clergy in particular, but opportunistic reflections dictated caution of action, because an open hostility would constitute a hindrance to reunion with the Eastern Orthodox Churches.[81]

The nineteenth century brought the hostility of the Roman authorities against Oriental married clergy into the open. In a decree dated September 16, 1835, Gregory XVI rejected the decisions of the Melchite Synod of Qarqafeh of 1806, which tried to give to the Melchite community a complete Church law. The

[77] See De Martinis, *op. cit.*, III, 227–228, §35–38.
[78] See E. Herman, *op. cit.*, pp. 153–154; J. Dauvillier, *op. cit.*, pp. 173, 177.
[79] De Martinis, *op. cit.*, III, 606, §22.
[80] See *ibid.*, III, 67, no. XXVI.
[81] See Wilhelm de Vries, *op. cit.*, p. 240.

decree is very hostile towards the Oriental Church law and traditions. Among other things it reproaches the Melchite Synod for the fact that it did not consider a celibate appropriate for village parishes in the East.[82]

In an instruction to the Rumanian Archbishop of Făgăras Alba-Julia dated March 24, 1858, the Sacred Congregation for the Propagation of Faith recommended celibacy in such strong terms that little or no room was left for married clergy. The argumentation runs as this: There is a necessity of unity in the Church, and therefore the difference of discipline in Oriental Churches may be preserved only in those matters which do not violate ecclesiastical decency. In consequence, the dignity of the priesthood seems to demand celibacy.[83]

This forceful Latinization and assimilation of the Oriental Church discipline regarding celibacy and married clergy, as well as many other matters of importance, was a blueprint of the new policy of the Roman Curia and an appropriate prelude to Vatican I, because the preparatory commission for the Eastern Church demanded the introduction of absolute clerical celibacy among the Orientals, and in support of this endeavor referred to the above-mentioned instruction of the Propaganda.[84] Moreover, the Latin-rite Patriarch Giuseppe Valerga in one of the sessions of the preparatory commission maintained that the Holy See had never approved the married clergy of Orientals, but only tolerated it. Now was the time to end this toleration, and therefore celibacy had to be introduced also in the Eastern Church.[85] Yet, since he had opportunity to see personally the situation in the East, he had to admit that it would be better to preserve the married clergy in the countryside of the Near East.[86] Fortunately, the Franco-German War prevented any formal decisions of the

[82] See Mansi XLVI, 685–812, 867–877; Fontes Series III, vol. VIII, 294.
[83] See *Collectanea S. Congregationis de Propaganda Fide*, I, Rome, 1907, 627 ff., no. 1158.
[84] See Mansi XLIX, 1013.
[85] See *ibid.*, 1002.
[86] See *ibid.*, 997.

First Vatican Council against the Oriental Christian heritage of the married clergy.

Under the pressure of the Roman Curia, several conferences and synods of the Catholic Oriental Churches which were held in the second half of the nineteenth century declared themselves in favor of the introduction of celibacy or even made it into a law. A very important factor behind these decisions was Pope Leo XIII himself, who was in general in favor of the retention of the Oriental discipline and traditions, but who precisely in matters concerning celibacy and married clergy, like his predecessors from the nineteenth century, believed in the necessity of assimiliating the Orientals to Latin absolute clerical celibacy.[87]

The first step in this direction was made under Pope Pius IX by the conference of Armenian bishops held in Rome in July of 1867. It advised each bishop to reduce the number of married priests in his diocese as far as possible and to encourage celibacy by all sensible means.[88] In 1888 the Syrian Catholic Synod of Sarfeh made celibacy into a law. However, the Patriarch could dispense from this law those who married before ordination to the subdiaconate. Also the married priests converting from the Jacobite Church should not be burdened with celibacy. Besides, the marriages of those in major orders was declared as null and void.[89] In 1898 the Synod of Catholic Copts which was celebrated in Alexandria carried exactly the same decisions.[90] However, the Synod of the Ukrainian Catholic Church (Ruthenian as it was called at that time by Rome) which was held in Lviv in 1891 restrained itself to general exhortations in favor of celibacy, without making it a law.[91]

But all this was only a prelude to the real fight which started

[87] See de Vries, *op. cit.*, p. 241.
[88] See Mansi XL, 957–958, art. 10.
[89] See *Synodus Sciarfensis Syrorum*, Rome, 1897, p. 202.
[90] See *Synodus Alexandrina Coptorum*, Rome, 1899, pp. 147–149.
[91] See C. Gatti-C. Korolevskij, *I riti e le chiese orientali*, I, Genoa, 1942, p. 57.

to take place in the twentieth century. First of all, the Roman Curia decided to restrict the remnants of the Catholic Oriental married clergy to the lands where they constitute a majority and to stop contamination of the celibatere Latin atmosphere with the presence of married Oriental clergy. To this effect the Congregation for the Propagation of Faith issued decrees in 1908[92] and 1913[93] that the Ruthenian priests who wish to minister in the United States and in Canada must be celibates or widowers without children. By a decree *Qua sollerti* dated December 23, 1929,[94] this prescription was extended to all Oriental priests who desired to minister to the faithful of their own rite in North and South America and Australia. In order to implement these decisions and to promote celibacy in Oriental lands, the Roman Curia devised a very shrewd tactic. Predominantly those were appointed to the episcopal office, in the Oriental Catholic Churches, who were in favor of an absolute clerical celibacy. The results were disastrous: some priests and many laymen revolted against these innovations and a real persecution of married clergy was in full swing at the time. Up to 200,000 faithful mainly of Ukrainian-Byzantine Rite in the U.S. and Canada left the Catholic Church and joined the Ukrainian Orthodox Church and some other Christian communities. Also the communists made fantastic gains. All this was a protest against an imposition of a foreign Church discipline.[95]

Similar events occured in the Ukraine, where between 1929[96] and World War II under the pressure of Rome almost only

[92] *AAS* 41 (1908), 3.
[93] *AAS* 5 (1913), 393 ff.
[94] *AAS* 22 (1930), 99–105.
[95] No formal study has been made of these events. The author of this article spoke with many witnesses of these events. Sporadic mention in the Ukrainian press can be found to the very present day, for example, Mykola Kornecjkyj, "Trahichni zanedbannia v U. K. Cerkvi," *Novy Shliakh*, Vol. XXXVIII, no. 38 (September 23, 1967), 8–9.
[96] In 1929 a conference of the Ukrainian and Ruthenian Catholic hierarchy took place in Rome. At least one session took place in the presence of Pope Pius XI. Evidently the pressure of the Roman Curia was very strong.

celibates were ordained. A major catastrophy was prevented by the prudence of the holy memory Metropolitan Andrii Sheptyts'kyj[97] who still permitted the ordination of some married candidates. Just the same, Orthodoxy and sectarianism were making rapid progress.

Ironically, the year 1929 witnessed also the beatification in the Basilica of St. Peter in Rome of "Der Gomidas Keumurgian, a married Armenian secular priest of Constantinople, who was put to death by the schismatics because of his unflinching preaching of the necessity of union with the Holy See."[98]

In 1957 Pius XII issued his famous apostolic letter *Cleri Sanctitati*, which contained one part of the new and general Church law for all Eastern Catholic Churches.[99] It repeated many traditional Oriental laws concerning married clergy and celibacy and stipulated that the particular law of each of the Oriental Catholic Churches should decide whether a married clergyman in minor orders may be admitted to subdiaconate and to the major orders. In those Oriental rites which do not admit married clergy in substance the Latin canon law is in effect.[100]

Among many references of the Second Vatican Council to the Oriental Churches we read in the *Decree on the Ministry and Life of the Priests*, article 16,[101] the following words: "It [i.e.,

[97] Concerning this great man see F. X. Murphy, *Sheptyts'kyi, Andrii*, NCE, XIII, 170–171.

[98] Clement C. Englert, *Eastern Catholics*, New York, 1940, p. 16.

[99] See note 47. Some Latinizing tendencies were also noticeable in this codification of the Oriental Church law, for example, canon 433, §1 begins with the words: 'Syncellus sit sacerdos caelebs . . .'" This is without any foundation in the Eastern canonical tradition.

[100] For example in the Malabar rite there exists only a rigid Latin concept of absolute clerical celibacy: see K. Mörsdorf, "Zölibat," *Lexikon für Theologie und Kirche*, X, Freiburg, 1965, 1398.

[101] This document was published on December 7, 1965. The English translation quoted is taken from *The Documents of Vatican II*, New York, 1966, p. 565. Cardinal Heenan tells us how this mention of married clergy came about: see *Council and Clergy*, London, 1966, p. 36:

The first speaker was Cardinal Meouchi, Maronite Patriarch of

perfect and perpetual continence on behalf of the kingdom of heaven] is not, indeed, demanded by the very nature of the priesthood, as is evident from the practice of the primitive Church and from the tradition of the Eastern Churches. In these Churches, in addition to all bishops and those others who by a gift of grace choose to observe celibacy, there also exist married priests of outstanding merit.

"While this most sacred Synod recommends ecclesiastical celibacy, it in no way intends to change that different discipline which lawfully prevails in Eastern Churches. It lovingly exhorts all those who have received the priesthood after marriage to persevere in their sacred vocation, and to continue to spend their lives fully and generously for the flock committed to them."

This very positive statement of Vatican II paved the way for a still more positive appreciation of the Eastern tradition of the married clergy expressed by Pope Paul VI in the encyclical *Sacerdotalis Caelibatus* cited at the beginning of this part of the

---

Antioch. He complained that the new schema, although very pleasing as an essay on the priesthood in general, failed because it reflected a purely western mentality. Except for a few brief insertions there was nothing in the schema which had particular reference to the life of priests in the Eastern Church and nothing at all which would help the married clergy. The schema was accurate enough when dealing with the timeless principles upon which the theology of the priesthood is based but it contained little which touched the actual lives of priests in the world today. He also complained that the outlook was restricted to the priest's work among Christians and had nothing to say about his mission to every creature to whom the Gospel by divine command had to be preached.

Evidently this was not acceptable to many. Cardinal Heenan, p. 37, reports that Cardinal Ruffini, Archbishop of Palermo, was heading in the opposite direction:

Referring to current rumours that there was some thought of abandoning clerical celibacy in the West he expressed thanks to the commission that the schema solemnly commended celibacy and drew attention to the fact that it is an outstanding reason for the excellence of the reputation of priests in the West and, by God's grace, is increasingly observed in the Eastern Church.

62

paper. And I think that we have to accept it as a starting point of any serious discussion concerning optional celibacy in the Latin Church. Then and only then does the whole document receive a new and fresh perspective for a more hopeful future.

III.

SOME THEOLOGICAL CONSIDERATIONS AND PRACTICAL CONCLUSIONS

Among the differences which exist between the Latin and the Eastern Church discipline, there is none which is better known by all than the one concerning celibacy and married clergy. This is only natural, because almost no legislation is of a more radical nature than celibacy, which tries to regulate the most intimate and personal sphere of existence of the very leaders of the Christian community. Yet, it reflects also very far-reaching theological views—for example, attitudes towards the world, created reality, marriage, sexuality, and so forth. It also generates very strong repercussions in the structure and life of the Christian community and to a very great extent determines its vitality and effectiveness. Therefore, let me present to you some reflections of the above-mentioned problematics.

It is clear that celibacy and major orders are not inseparably linked by divine command, but by ecclesial legislation only. Therefore, this legislation can and must be revised and updated theologically and practically both in the East and the West. There remains, however, a crucial and decisive problem, namely, the distinction between absolute clerical celibacy and virginity,[102]

102 On sacred virginity see Eduard Freiherr von der Goltz, Λόγος σωτηρίας προς τήν παρθενον (*De virginitate*) *eine echte Schrift des Athanasius*, Leipzig, 1905; Hugo Koch, *Virgines Christi: Die Gelübde der Gottgeweihten Jungfrauen in den ersten drei Jahrhunderten*, Leipzig, 1967; St. Ambrose, *De virginibus*, Bonn, 1933; Dietrich von Hildebrand, *In*

which are explicitly or implicitly confused in the Latin Church and partly even in Eastern Christianity. Besides, many elements of the sacrament of order and of sacred virginity were artificially included in the concept of clerical celibacy. One of the sources of confusion is the fact that an absolute clerical celibacy includes, of course, many true charismatic virgins who also received a vocation and charism to the priesthood, but includes on the other hand many of those who received a true vocation to the priesthood but not to virginity and who had to reject their vocation to the sacrament of marriage in order to become priests.[103] Moreover, the defenders of an absolute clerical celibacy point to the charismatic virgins who received sacred orders and proclaim them to be true clerical celibates. However, all those who are incontinent are usually labelled not as bad celibates but as bad priests.[104] All this betrays a deep confusion of concepts and realities that must be rectified. Therefore, in the last analysis it is necessary to consider a complex of four different realities: the sacrament of marriage, the sacrament of order, celibacy, and

---

Defence of Purity: An Analysis of the Catholic Ideals of Purity and Virginity, London, 1945: W. Schöllgen, "Zum Problem der Jungfräulichkeit in der Lehte Jesu," *Anima,* 7 (1952), 201–207; A. Löhr, "Die Jungfräulichkeit als christliche Wesenshaltung nach Schrift und Liturgie," *ibid.,* 207–220; L. M. Weber, "Jungfräulichkeit und Theologie," *ibid.,* 220–227; Pius XII, "Sacra virginitas" (*AAS* 46, 1954, 175 ff.); Romano Guardini, *Ehe und Jungfräulichkeit,* Mainz, 1956; J. Blinzler, εἰσὶν εὐνοῦχοι, *Zeitschrift für die neutestamentliche Wissenschaft und die Kunde der älteren Kirche,* 48 (1957), 254–270; J. G. Ziegler, *Antike Enthaltung und christliche Jungfräulichkeit,* Würzburg, 1959; Johann Michl-Leonhard Weber, "Jungfräulichkeit," *Lexikon für Theologie und Kirche,* III (1959), 1245–1250; Karl Rahner, "Zur Theologie der Entsagung," *Schriften zur Theologie,* III, Zürich, 1961, pp. 61–72; A. Auer, "Jungfräulichkeit," *Handbuch theologischer Begriffe,* I, Munich, 1962, pp. 771–777; Werner Kettloff, "Jungfräulichkeit," *Wahrheit und Zeugnis,* Düsseldorf, 1964, pp. 443–449; Karl Rahner, "Über die evangelischen Räte," *Geist und Leben,* 17 (1964), 17–37; P. T. Camelot, "Virginity," *NCE,* XIV, 701–704.

[103] An example of this case can be found in Gabriel Longo, *Spoiled Priest,* New Hyde Park, New York, 1966.

[104] For example, in the encyclical "Sacerdotalis caelibatus" of Pope Paul VI in 83–90.

64

sacred virginity. For didactic reasons we shall compare primarily virginity with absolute clerical celibacy, including occasionally the sacraments of order and marriage as the points of reference. However, in this comparison we have to keep in mind the relativity of the images and symbols by which we shall try to describe the above mentioned realities, and the fact that it is an Eastern theologian meditating upon them.

Since the very beginning of Christianity the charism of virginity quite rightly enjoys the highest respect and to a certain extent also spiritual authority in the Church. Therefore, all defenders of an absolute clerical celibacy willingly or unwillingly draw arguments which can be used for the defense of virginity only and in many cases describe not celibacy but virginity. Since this became all too evident to modern scholarly research, the defenders of an absolute clerical celibacy in the Latin Church started to fabricate new and artificial concepts and distinctions. Among them we find a distinction between priestly virginity and monastic or lay virginity.[105] Some theologians tried to substantiate this distinction with a claim that priestly virginity is an assimilation to or an imitation of Christ the virgin and mediator between God and man. Through this priestly virginity the Latin priest, like the second Christ, dedicates himself to Christ's bride, the Church. On the other hand, monastic or lay virginity represents the bridal state of the Church in respect to Christ. Priestly virginity is a Christological one oriented towards the Church and the ministry. Monastic or lay virginity is oriented towards the Christ and God.[106]

It is clear, however, that the Oriental Churches never made or accepted any such distinction, because there is no evidence to it in the Bible or tradition, which for Oriental Christians is not a

---

[105] The best example of this is Wilhelm Bertrams, *Der Zölibat des Priesters*, Würzburg, 1962.

[106] On the criticism of these views see *Catholicus, Um den Zölibat: Eine Studie und Diskussionsgrundlage*, Zurich, 1966, pp. 67–72.

past but present and vivifying reality. Virginity in the Bible indeed is one and undivided.[107] It is, as far as its contents and terminology are concerned, a biblical and traditional good. It cannot be legislated, because it is a grace or a gratuitous gift of God given freely to whom he will. Therefore, all the Church can do is to legislate the protection of virginity and of virgins and of their proper place within the Christian community, but always in accordance with the Bible. Celibacy, on the other hand, is a canonical term and concept, and we know all too well that it can be legislated upon.

Sacred virginity is a positive term of integrity, freedom, and above all openness to the Triadic God, because it is by its very nature oriented to God the Father, through the Son and in the Holy Spirit. Celibacy is a negative term (*celebs* in Latin meaning "alone" or "single"). It includes within its concept two distinct moments: first, canonical incapacity to receive the sacrament of marriage, and second, a prohibition of any sexual intercourse, or a "perfect chastity," as it is being called, with an emphasis on the biological or material aspect, in many cases to the detriment of the social or spiritual aspects. It is oriented towards the practical ends, especially the service or ministry in the Church and the alleged freedom of its exercise.[108]

The most important distinction, however, is the fact that virginity is a charism or a free gift of the Holy Spirit given from above. It connotes a special unity of action with the Spirit on the part of the virgin for the benefit of a personal sanctification and an edification of the body of Christ, which since the day of the Pentecost is indwelled by the Holy Spirit. On the other hand, celibacy is a positive ecclesiastical but human law, that is, it originates not from above, but from below. It comes from a positive will of a human ecclesial authority which requires more

107 *Ibid.*, pp. 17–29.
108 On the canonical meaning of celibacy in the Latin Church see Klaus Mörsdorf, *Lehrbuch des Kirchenrechts*, I, Munich, 1959, pp. 271–274.

66

of priests than the positive will of God expressed in divine revelation.

It is also very important to note that sacred virginity is an eschatological sign in itself independent of any sacrament. It is analogous to baptism by blood of a martyr unbaptized by water, which has in itself the efficacy of a sacrament of baptism by water, that is, justification, sanctification, divinization, incorporation into Christ and his Church, and the inchoative eschatological fulfillment[109] Celibacy by contrast is an artificial addition to the sacrament of order, or practically speaking it is a *conditio sine qua non* in the Latin Church which stands in opposition to the sacrament of marriage. Thus virginity is primarily a pneumatic or spiritual sign of being open to and being united mystically with God, whereas celibacy is too often an artificially constructed somatic or bodily sign of being unmarried. Therefore, we can describe virginity as a mystical marriage with the divine reality and self-fulfillment in joy, and the three theological virtues of faith, hope, and love. Celibacy by contrast is a highly mythologized abstension from the sacrament of marriage usually without any real joy or self-fulfillment.

Pursuing further our meditation we can say that virgins constitute a special spiritual order in the Church, but no caste or ruling class. Unfortunately, absolute clerical celibacy by its very nature tends to establish a priestly ruling class or a closed caste of unmarried men in charge of the Church.

It is true that in the past a married clergy has often developed into a closed caste, for example through the inheritance of parishes or even bishoprics from father to son, and that the introduction of celibacy was partly a reaction against this fact.[110] That, however, is no longer an argument against a married

---

[109] See Werner Dettloff, *Jungfräulichkeit, in Wahrheit und Zeugnis,* Düsseldorf, 1964, pp. 448–449.

[110] For example, in the Armenian Church in the fourth and fifth centuries the bishoprics were inherited from the father by the son. See de Vries, *op. cit.,* Freiburg, 1963, p. 11.

clergy since in modern society people no longer inherit automatically their father's position. An option and balance between married and celibate clergy would tend to prevent both the sociological priestly caste of the past and the spiritual type of today.

True virginity is a sign of a spiritual maturity which, as pointed out above, realizes itself in a spiritual or mystical marriage. An absolute clerical celibacy, on the other hand, includes true virgins but also in many instances (which are well known to us) it is a sign of spiritual immaturity and personal infantilism. Sacred virginity represents spiritual childhood of God and a very special spiritual brotherhood or sisterhood in respect to fellow men, whereas absolute clerical celibacy is an attempt to represent a spiritual fatherhood which in fact is a prerogative of the sacrament of order or priesthood and as such has nothing to do with celibacy.[111]

In order to be dispensed of clerical celibacy a Latin-rite presbyter today has to prove to his superiors and judges a serious mental disorder or homosexuality, whereas a normal heterosexual man constituted in clerical celibacy, who falls in love and receives from the Holy Spirit a desire for the sacrament of marriage and a Christian witness through his Christian marriage to the unbelieving world, gets no dispensation from his superiors. In my opinion, ecclesiastical superiors sin against the Holy Spirit and the human dignity of their fellow priest in this regard. All this means that celibacy under normal circumstances is conceived as a permanent state, whereas virginity according to the prompting of the Spirit can be either a permanent or a temporary gift. Yet, virginity by its very nature is diametrically opposed to the sacrament of marriage, whereas in the priesthood or the sacrament of orders no such radical opposition exists, as the Bible and the legislation of the Eastern Church prove.

[111] See *Aperçus sur la paternité spirituelle dans la tradition orthodoxe: Contacts*, Anne XIX, no. 158.

68

Sacred virginity is a vocation expressed by God, which tries to establish a vertical relationship to God primarily for the benefit of the person himself. Clerical celibacy is a vocation expressed by the Church authority which tries to establish a horizontal binding primarily for the benefit of the Church. As the result, celibacy is obsessed with practical and economical considerations, whereas virginity as such has nothing to do with any of them.

An absolute clerical celibacy to my mind in many instances is a hidden or clandestine Semi-Pelagianism, because often it is presented as if it were based on a decision of man and a vocation by the Church, which promises cooperation of God to those who make the right decision to become a priest. In other words, in theory the Latins usually admit that there are two different vocations, one to celibacy and one to the priesthood. In practice, however, they are trying desperately to inculcate into the minds of the seminarians and priests that a real vocation to the priesthood includes also a vocation to celibacy. Sacred virginity, on the other hand, is a call and a grace of God which requires a cooperation of man and not vice versa.

Finally, an absolute clerical celibacy of the Latin Church and some Latinized Uniate Churches of the East is an anti-ecumenical legislation which is a barrier to reunion and a sign of a feeling of superiority of the Latins over all others who admit married clergy in their communities. Sacred virginity is an element of the Christian unity, because it is witnessed to in the Bible and is common to most Christian communities.[112]

This rather schematically presented comparison between sacred virginity and clerical celibacy can serve us, I believe, as a foundation for a serious discussion.

Unfortunately, today in the Latin Church we are witnessing a very rapid devaluation of sacred virginity and of monastic life.

[112] The best example of revival of monastic life among the Protestant brethren is the community of Taizé. Sub-prior of the community Max Thurian wrote *Marriage and Celibacy,* London, 1959.

69

It is a very unfortunate and destructive phenomenon which must be remedied at all costs. However, to an impartial observer it is clear that one of the factors nowadays which degrades sacred virginity is a great number of bad clerical celibates. It is also clear that both sacred virginity and the integrity of the Christian community (including the monastic community) must be protected against them. Therefore, from an Eastern point of view it is much more logical to admit to the sacred ministry married men of good moral standing and reputation, than to take chances with an absolute clerical celibacy and its possible evil consequences. Thus as far back as 1274 a synod of the Eastern Slavs of Byzantine rite stipulated that only married men were to be ordained as secular priests.[113] All those who desired to become secular unmarried priests had to receive a very special permission to do so. This is so, because the sacrament of orders is there primarily as a help and foundation of the sacramental riches and divinized life of the Church of Christ and secondarily as a foundation of a juridical and hierarchical structure of the Church. An absolute clerical celibacy always tended to upset this balance and is mainly responsible for the all too worldly representation of the Church as a monarchical and hierarchical institution.

Now let me formulate a few practical conclusions concerning celibacy and married clergy, which to my mind should be kept in front of the whole of Christianity in any meaningful discussion or renewal.

(1) Sacred virginity must be protected as a biblical good and a gift of God. As an eschatological sign it must be placed in its proper dignified position in the charismatic life of the Church.

(2) Monastic life must come again into its own as a community of virgins, who are living an intense life of prayer, penance, and sacrifice, but not in fear of or in hostility towards

---

[113] See Pfliegler, *op. cit.*, pp. 27–28.

70

the world, but in love of the whole extra-divine reality and in active promotion of God's kingdom, that is, salvation, transfiguration, sanctification, divinization, and inchoative eschatological fulfillment of the whole extra-divine reality.

(3) Virginal secular priests should be a rare but honorable and cherished exception. Generally, secular clergy should be married. By the sacrament of marriage and possibly by the charism of good fatherhood to their children, the married clergymen should witness to the unbelieving and the believing world of the sacredness of marriage and its typological significance as the image of the kingdom of God.

(4) The most important area which requires a special study and an appropriate solution concerns the wives of priests and their children.[114] Special schools for the wives of priests or at least some special courses would be very desirable. Also ordination of some of the wives of priests to the lay, non-hierarchical office of deaconess in certain cases would open new avenues in the ministry of the Church.[115]

(5) The texts of St. Paul, 1 Timothy 3, 12 and Titus 1f. concerning deacons and bishops who were to be "married but once" should be interpreted as a counsel and not as a strict command. Therefore, the sacrament of marriage, virginity, and chaste widowhood must be set free as options to all clergymen at all times. This means that a deacon, priest, or bishop (the Pope not excluded) should be free to choose the virginal or married state, or first or second marriage after ordination, or separation from his wife with her consent at any time before or after ordination and eventual reunion of the two, or chaste widowhood before or after ordination after the wife's death. All these options must be left to a free and mature Christian deci-

---

[114] See William Douglas, *Ministers' Wives*, New York, 1965.
[115] See Karl Rahner-Herbert Vorgrimler, *Diakonia in Christo: Über die Erneuerung des Diakonates*, Freiburg, 1962, *passim*.

sion of each of the members of the clergy in accordance with the dictates of their conscience and the promptings of the Holy Spirit.

I hope that the time will come when the Church universal can rejoice because God has sent her a virginal pope, and during a following pontificate she will rejoice because a great spiritual leader and a great married personality with a saintly wife and good believing children has been sent to her by God as her visible head.

hryhorij skovoroda - philosopher or theologian?

"The world was after me, but never trapped me."

1.IX.1722 — 29.X.1794

Originally published in *The New Review. A Journal of East-European History*, 13 (1973), pp.50–61; reprinted here with permission.

HRYHORIJ SKOVORODA — PHILOSOPHER OR THEOLOGIAN?*

Petro B. T. Bilaniuk
University of St. Michael's College
in the University of Toronto

True scholarly research must strive to rectify or complete accepted scholarly, scientific, or popular views. In fact, one of its most important tasks is constant verification, perfection, and development of the heritage of knowledge. It is therefore often necessary to perform a somewhat radical evaluation of conclusions of various branches of knowledge, or to compose a fuller and more extact characterization of an individuaĺ, or to elucidate the creativity and heritage of a personage in scholarship, art, social and political life, etc. Such evaluation, of course, often necessitates correction or even rejection of antiquated views. Or it introduces classification closer to objective reality and not tinted nor dictated by an ideology accepted a **priori,** by philosophical or scientific systems, nor by other purely subjective motives.

This paper is a result of such considerations and of initial investigation of the character and literary heritage of Hryhorij Skovoroda. This figure, who is certainly the most distinguished and most original Ukrainian thinker, is characterized by almost all scholarly and popular publications as a "philosopher" and the "founder of the so-called philosophy of the heart"[1], a Western mystic in Ukraine[2], a writer[3], etc.

The most absurd evaluation of Hryhorij Skovoroda is proposed by the "Soviet scholarship", which tendentiously claims that "philosophical views of Skovoroda evolved in the direction of materialism and were characterized by a constantly sharper presentation of social problems and a striving to definitively liberate himself from the bondage of idealism and religion."[4]

The last authoritative word of free Ukrainian scholarship on this subject was a brief characterization of Hryhorij Skovoroda by I. Mirtschuk:[5]

The greatest Ukrainian philosopher was Gregory Skovoroda (1722 - 94), a contemporary of Kant; his influence spread to other Slavic countries. Born into a Kozak family in the province of Poltava, he studied at the Kiev Academy and later abroad, in Vienna, Munich, and Breslau. Skovoroda, who is generally known as the "Ukrainian Socrates", wrote his works in the form of dialogues and made a profound anthropologism the source of his philosophical contemplation. To him man is the greatest riddle in life, and self-knowledge the most important means for its solution. The philosophical system of Skovoroda embraces three aspects: the ontological, the cognitive, and the ethical. According to him, man is a microcosm reflecting the macrocosm. In order to get to know the universe one must first know man, that is, oneself. Self-knowledge, therefore, was for Skovoroda the first aim of philosophy which he approached with the Socratic maxim "Know thyself." The universe had two aspects for him, one visible and material which was worthless, and the other invisible and spiritual, which was of inestimable value and to which alone man's life should be dedicated. However, the search for truth is not an end in itself, but only a means which prompts us to exercise our wills and to use our hearts. The great value of Skovoroda's philosophy lies, therefore, not in his theoretical speculations, but in his practical quest for happiness. It is happiness, which, according to Skovoroda, is the aim of our lives; not, however, the happiness which results from material satisfaction, but that which comes to us when we fulfil our inner quest, and, through it, God's will. Thus self-knowledge and living one's life according to the natural order and therefore in accord with God are the major premises of Skovoroda's thought. He was a keen student of the Bible which he carried with him wherever he went.

The remark concerning Skovoroda's unceasing love of Sacred Scripture is of great importance.[6] Was Skovoroda a philosopher or a theologian?

The fundamental distinction between theology and philosophy can be reduced to the mode of knowledge and to the fount of truth. The theologian discerns the acceptance of the divine self-revelation (the word-revelation) through the gift of faith and with a human intellectual and natural knowledge. The philosopher discerns only a human natural and intellectual knowledge which extends to the world and its phenomena (the work-revelation), but without the explicit intervention of the divine self-revelation (that is, without the word-revelation). In philosophy, therefore, God is only a Supreme Being, the Creator and the All-Ruler of the natural world, and thus the Author of natural truth. True philosophy may not deny **a priori** the existence of God the Creator, or of God the Giver of grace and of the work- or word-revelation. On the contrary, philosophy can and should attempt to elucidate by rational arguments the existence of God the Creator and the possibility, or even the probability, of the divine self-revelation by the inspired word. It is, however, only the believing man who, without any apodictic and compelling arguments and under the influence of the divine light of faith, arrives at the existence of God as the giver of divine life, light, and love. Such an act of faith surpasses the merely philosophical and natural act of knowing or speculation, and attains to super-rational and salvational reality.[7]

On the basis of the exposition above, we can affirm that both sciences of theology and philosophy are fundamental sciences which may not conflict with one another, because God is the ultimate ground of both the inner-Triadic and the extra-divine reality and truth. Moreover, history is an eloquent witness that theology constantly has used the contemporary philosophy as an auxiliary source of knowledge and as an instrument for deeper and more exact penetration and elucidation of the divinely revealed truths. This is so because the divine love and salvational self-revelation are addressed to the whole man as a complete person, with body and soul, with intellect, will, and feelings; that is, with all metaphysical and integral parts and aspects.[8]

When we apply the above elaborations, classifications and divisions to the person and heritage of Hryhorij Skovoroda, there emerges an entirely new image of this extraordinary figure. First of all, those who classify Skovoroda as a philosopher would agree that he was not a systematic philosopher; that is, he did not contruct a coherent system which would do justice to all branches and divisions of philosophy. They would also agree that his main interest was in the area of axiology (with an emphasis on ethics and philosophy of religion) and in philosophy as **Weltanschauung** (with an emphasis on anthropology and theodicy). Also it is not sufficient to mention Skovoroda's love for Sacred Scripture. To him the Bible was the main source of the divine self-revelation, and usually served as the starting point of his thinking. The Bible also was to him the definitive authority and the rule of truth. This indicates that Skovoroda was concerned primarily with the divinely revealed truth, which to him was a divine gift, accessible only on account of divine faith. Therefore, it is necessary to classify Skovoroda primarily as a theologian or a Christian thinker, and only secondarily as a philosopher, writer, poet, etc.

These statements are relatively easy to prove. Almost every major work of Skovoroda begins with a short introduction or introductory chapter entitled, "the consistency of the discourse",[9] "the main subject-matter of this book",[10] "the foundation of the dialogue",[11] "the foundation",[12] "this book's main subject",[13] "main subject of the work",[14] "the main subject and consistency of the booklet",[15] or "the foundation of the parable".[16] Each of these introductions consists of biblical quotations which constitute the main thoughts or themes, as well as the main arguments in favor of the author's conclusions. Often his work opens with an appropriate biblical quotation which serves as the guideline of the whole work in question.[17] Also, all of his writings are rich with scriptural quotations which serve as the foundation and guideline of his dialogue and reasoning.

The "Garden of Divine Songs Sprouting Forth from the Seeds of the Sacred Scripture"[18] is a characteristically Skovorodian work. It is a cycle of thirty religious poems based on biblical themes. Each poem opens with a verse from Sacred Scripture which serves as the foundation of that "song". The content of these poems does not leave any doubt in the reader's mind that a theologian and moralist is speaking to him. A very characteristic example is the fifth stanza of the twenty-sixth song:[19]

> O Christ, the sacred fountain of graces!
> Pour Thy Spirit upon the shepherd.
> Be unto him an Archetype,
> So that gazing upon him,
> Each man of his flock may be led to act,
> And so extend his blessed life-span.

One of the most eloquent witnesses to the exalted role of the Bible in Skovoroda's thought and life is a quotation from an article, "Kinship to Theology", in one of his fundamental works entitled "Dialogue, Called the Alphabet, or a Primer of Peace":[20]

Flee from anxiety, embrace solitude, love lowliness, kiss purity, befriend suffering, study sacred languages, learn at least one well, and become one of the scribes [-scholars] educated for the divine kingdom, of whom Christ [said]: "So then every scribe instructed in the kingdom of h[eaven is like a householder who bringeth forth from his storeroom things new and old. Matt. 13, 52]..." That is why these scribes are learning languages. Be not afraid! Hunger, cold, hatred, persecution, denigration, abuse, and all effort is not only tolerable, but also sweet, provided that thou wert born for it. Thy Lord is thy strength. All this will make thee much keener and much more sublime. A torrent in nature, be it a rushing stream or a flame, courseth much more quickly through a narrow passage. Greet the ancient pagan philosophers. Converse with the universal Fathers [of the Church]. Finally, thou shalt come into the Israelite land, to Bethlehem itself, into the house of bread and wine, into the most sacred temple of the Bible, chanting with David: "I rejoiced because they said unto me [: We will go into the house of the Lord".] (Ps. 121, 1)... How cautiously one must enter this wedding hall! Be well dressed! Wash thy hands and feet. Then sit down at this immortal table. But beware! Do not push [thy hand] into the salt-dish with the host. Remember that this is not thine, nor a carnal meal, but the one of the Lord. God beware thee! Thou shalt die if thou eatest blood. Eat the blood and the body of the Lord and not thine own. "May this be good and pleasing unto thee before thy Lord God [?]" Receive, but [only] from the Lord; eat, but [only] for the Lord; be satisfied, but [only] before the Lord.

This description of a theological training reads like an autobiographical account of Hryhorij Skovoroda himself, and quite clearly demonstrates that in the final analysis he is a theologian. Different stages of this training are: 1. the acquisition of the necessary virtues, above all, patience and persistence; 2. the acquisition of knowledge of the sacred tongues (Hebrew, Greek, Latin); 3. an acquaintance with pagan philosophers (especially Socrates, Plato, Aristotle); 4. dialogue with the Church Fathers; and finally, 5. entrance into "the sacred temple of the Bible", which opens the door to the highest mystery of the Body and Blood of the Lord; that is, the Holy Eucharist.

The theological thinking of Skovoroda emerges very clearly also in his works dealing with purely secular themes. The preface to "The Tales of Kharkiw",[21] for example, witnesses to the theological intention of the author. He wishes to illustrate with human examples the divine truths revealed in the Bible.[22] As a result, the moral teaching deduced from each of the tales (the so-called "strength") is theological in nature, or at least contains a very theological ingredient. It is also interesting to note that there, too, we find quotations from Holy Scripture, especially in the "strength" of the last tale.[23]

Skovoroda also quite clearly distinguished between the natural and the supernatural modes of knowledge; that is, between the natural act of faith based on reason and intuition, and the supernatural act of the divine faith. This is clearly indicated in his work "The Initial Door to Christian Morality", where in chapter two, entitled "On Universal Faith", he writes:[24] "Similarly, all ages and nations have always unanimously believed that there is some mystery; namely, a power which is poured out upon everything and which dominates all things." Again in the sixth chapter, entitled "On the True Faith", Skovoroda writes:[25] "It [i.e., true faith] is a beatitude which is hidden from all counsel and which [acts] as if it were looking from afar through a telescope, with which it is also portrayed." For Skovoroda, purity of heart is not a naturally acquired quality, but a "calm breathing and blowing in the soul of the Holy Spirit";[26] that is, a supernatural gift or a charisma.

The last statement introduces a new cycle of questions concerning Skovoroda's famous "philosophy of heart", of which some scholars consider him to be the founder.[27] The most profound and the best known statement of Skovoroda concerning the heart of man, or his cordocentric philosophy, is contained at the beginning of his work, "The Initial Door to Christian Morality". Together with the immediate context, this text reads:[28]

Thanks be unto blessed God that He made the necessary [things] easy, and the difficult [things] unnecessary.

There is nothing sweeter and nothing more necessary for man than happiness; also there is nothing easier than that. Thanks be unto blessed God.

The divine Kingdom is within us. Happiness in the heart, the heart in love, and love in the law of the Eternal [God].

This is the perpetually fine weather and the never-setting sun illuminating the darkness of the heart's abysses. Thanks be unto blessed God.

Skovoroda's thoughts concerning the human heart are much more clearly outlined in his work "Narcissus". There, in one of the dialogues of Cleopas with his Friend, we read:[29]

Friend: ... "The divine Word, His counsels and **thoughts**, these constitute a plan, incomprehensibly extending unto all [things] in the whole earth, containing all [things] and fulfilling all [things]. This is the depth of His riches and wisdom. And what can overflow more fully than thoughts? O heart, an abyss wider than all waters and the sky [itself]! ... How deep thou art! Thou encompassest and containest all, and nothing can accommodate thee."

Cleopas: "Verily I recall the following statement of Jeremiah: 'Profound is the heart of man, more than anything else, and man is...[?]'"

Friend: "Lo, this man encompasseth all. He strengtheneth thy bodily hands and feet. He is the head and strength of thine eyes and ears. And if thou canst believe him, 'Thine eyes shall not be obscured and thy lips shall not disintegrate unto the ages of ages.'"[?]

Cleopas: "I believe and I compel my heart to the obedience of faith. But is it not possible to strengthen me at least a little? Please do not be offended. The higher I ascend in the comprehension of invisibility, the stronger will be my faith."

Friend: "Thou askest rightly, because God can accept neither our prayers nor sacrifices if we do not recognize Him. Love Him and always draw closer to Him; with thy heart and knowledge draw closer to Him, and not by outward feet and mouth. Thy heart is the head of thine inner self. And if it is the head, then thou thyself art thy heart. But if thou wilt not draw closer to and bind thyself with Him who is the **head** of thy **head**, then thou wilt remain a dead shadow and a cadaver. If there is a body above the body, then there is [also] a head above the head, and over the old [there is] the **new heart**. Oh, should we not be ashamed and sorry that God asketh us for a commitment and getteth it not?"

On the basis of these two texts it is possible to outline a brief synthesis of Skovoroda's teaching concerning the human heart. "Heart", first of all, is the emotional organ of man, or the seat of feelings and happiness. Briefly, it constitutes the internal dimension or aspect of man. However, just as the human being (which according to the teaching of Skovoroda is a microcosm) is an incomprehensible and immeasurable mystery, so too his heart is an immeasurable and all-embracing mystery. This concept of "heart" is closely linked with the intellectual aspect of man. It is possible to say that "heart" is the intellectual, voluntary, and emotional center or "head" of the human person. As such it represents the seat of a person's moral life and thus is a seat of happiness. It is also the heart which is the seat of the "divine kingdom within us"; that is, it is the first object or dimension of the sanctification of man under the influence of divine grace. And this is why Skovoroda distinguishes between the "old" and the "new" heart; namely, between a sinful man and the divinely sanctified person. Thus in the teaching of Skovoroda the heart is not simply a physical or biological organ which performs an important physiological function, but an ancient and a realistic symbol of some aspects of a very complex human being. Moreover, "heart" is that dynamic foundation of human existence from which man always draws self-knowledge. Therefore this self-knowledge can be found in the heart alone, even though it remains always imperfect and unsatisfactory. Moreover, in Skovoroda's teaching "heart" sometimes approaches the meaning of conscience and of the meeting place between God and man.

But is this teaching of Skovoroda concerning the heart an original one? Is it, consequently, possible to term him "the founder of the so-called philosophy of heart"? The appearance of biblical quotations from the book of the prophet Jeremiah indicates that

Skovoroda consciously drew his information concerning the heart from the Bible. By the same token, he relied in his thinking on ancient Hebrew metaphysics and anthropology. Concurrently, his thoughts concerning the metaphysical parts of man and his theory of knowledge remind one of the Neo-Platonic and Hellenistic theories of Plotinus, who recast the thoughts of Plato.

One of the tasks of those scholars concerned with Skovoroda's writings should be to investigate the theological and biblical literature contemporary with him in order to establish the extent of its influence on his cordocentric thought. Nevertheless, a very short synthesis of the biblical teaching concerning the heart already casts new light on the teaching of Skovoroda:[30] The Hebrew word "lev" (a more recent form of "levav") means primarily an organ of the human body (Os. 13, 8) or a seat of the biological life of man (Is. 1, 6). However, the term "heart" in the Bible is used most often in a metaphysical sense; that is, as an inner aspect of man, the center of his being, the seat of man's attitude towards life and of his moral conduct. This is why the Hebrew mode of thought ascribes to "heart" not only feelings and emotional activity (Num. 15, 39; Deut. 28, 47; Ps. 76, 6; Os. 11, 8; etc.), but also activities of thinking and willing. Thus thoughts rise to the heart (Is. 65, 17; Jer. 3, 16; 7, 31); good and evil thoughts dwell in the heart (Ps. 73, 7; Dan. 2, 30; Esdras 38, 10); in the heart man converses with himself (Gen. 17, 17; Deut. 7, 17). Into the heart of man God deposits wisdom (1 Kings 10, 24; Ps. 90, 12), which is the beginning of planning and of decision (Ex. 35, 5; 36, 2; I Sam. 14, 7; Est. 7, 5). In the heart is rooted the religious attitude of man (1 Sam. 12, 25; Jer. 32, 40; Prov. 3, 5; Neh. 9, 8). The conversion of man to God takes place in the heart (Joel 2, 12; I Kings 8, 47) and in it conscience speaks (I Sam. 25, 31).

It is possible to develop this synthesis further and to illustrate it with examples from the New Testament also. It would also be very profitable to institute a minutely detailed comparison between the biblical and the Skovorodian teaching on "heart". The few remarks above indicate clearly, however, the true source of Skovoroda's teaching on the heart. Thus it is legitimate to conclude that in Skovoroda's heritage there is no strictly philosophical teaching on the heart, but rather a discursive theological elaboration of the biblical teaching, combined with philosophical elements borrowed principally from ancient Stoic thought.

The thought of Hryhorij Skovoroda is, then, almost entirely a **terra ignota** which must be investigated primarily by theologians. This is so because Skovoroda is not, strictly speaking, a philosopher, but a moral theologian and a Christian thinker. Scholars with an exclusively philosophical and literary training will be confused by this great person, or will wander about aimlessly through his writings, as they have been doing ever since his own day.

NOTES

* Adapted from the Ukrainian "Hryhorij Skovoroda — filosof chy bohoslov?" in **Bohoslovja** 34 (1970), 244-253; reprinted in **Zbirnyk nauko-vykh pracị na poshanu Jevhena Wertyporocha...** (Toronto, 1971) 55-65. Sincere thanks are due to Marjorie Boyle, M.A., who corrected the English and prepared the manuscript of this report for publication.

1 "This period also boasts the greatest Ukrainian philosopher Hryhory Skovoroda (1722-94), founder of the so-called 'philosophy of the heart' and author of 30 fairy tales." G. Luznycky and L. D. Rudnytzky, "Ukrainian Literature", in: **New Catholic Encyclopedia,** New York etc., 1967), XIV, 370.

2 A. Schmaus, "Dichtung", in: **Lexicon für Theologie und Kirche,** Freiburg i. Br., 1959², III, 367: Die rel. Barocklyrick kommt auch bei Tsche-chen (B. Bridel), westl. Mystik in der Ukraine (Skovoroda) zu Wort."

3 A brief but tendentious, and Marxist-Leninist, history of the in-vestigations of the personage and writings of H. Skovoroda can be found in M. Redjko, **Svitohlad H. S. Skovorody** (Vydavnyctvo Lvivsjkoho Univer-sytetu, 1967) 3-20, with a selected bibliography on Skovoroda in the foot-notes.

4 D. Kh. Ostrjanyn, P. M. Popov, and I. A. Tabachnykov in an essay, "Vydatnyj ukrajinsjkyj filosof i pysjmennyk", published in: Hryhorij Sko-voroda, **Tvory u dvokh tomakh** (Kyjiv, 1961), 1, xiii. There we also read: "The representatives of the dominating classes have made an all-out effort to use the writings of the great professor against the feudal society for the defence of the feudal-landlordly system, the absolute monarchy and the church-establisment. They have perverted the true views of the thinker and presented him as a mystic and a theologian. Stressing the theological form and religious phraseology, with the help of which Skovoroda most of the time expressed his moral-ethical principles of 'universal love', 'self-knowledge', 'self-perfectioning', the bourgeois scholars rejected or obscured the concrete social questions which were raised by the philosopher, his angry and passionate fight against parasitism, profiteering, the official

religion, the clergy, the rich, the nobles and the bureaucrats; they denied the democratism of the philosopher and his burning patriotism." The same views were expressed by Ivan Pilchuk, "Poet-myslytel. Estetychni pohlady H. Skovorody", in: H. Skovoroda, **Poeziji** (Kyjiv, 1971) 3-44; Pavlo Tychyna, "Hryhorij Skovoroda" in: **Skovoroda** Symfonija (Kyjiv, 1961) 348-363; Borys Derkach, "Narodnyj filosof, poet-humanist", in: Hryhorij Skovoroda, **Vy-brani tvory** (Kyjiv, 1971) 5-19.

⁵ Volodymyr Kubijovyč, ed., **Ukraine: A Concise Encyclopedia** (Toronto, 1963) 955-956. The final paragraph in the Ukrainian edition of the same work reads: "Finally it is necessary to recall his love of Sacred Scripture, which constantly accompanied the Ukrainian Socrates during his wandering through this world." **Encyklopedija Ukrajinoznavstva,** V. Kubijovyč and Z. Kuzela, eds., (Munich-New York, 1949) 721. A very interesting and precise description of Skovoroda and his period can be found in Mykhajlo Hrushevskyj, **Z istoriji relihijnoji dumky na Ukrajini** (Winnipeg-Munich-Detroit, 1962) 104-112. Jevhen Onackyj, **Ukrajinska Mala Encyclopedija** (Buenos Aires, 1957...), 1758, writes: "SKOVORODA HRYHORIJ (1722-1794) — famous, but not very well investigated, philosopher whose works were not published during his life, because the contemporary censorship found them to be 'contrary to the Holy Scriptures and insulting to the monastic orders'. Skovoroda was educated in the spirit of philosophical and religious studies and, basing his philosophical thought on the Bible, he kept on rebelling against the dead ecclesiastical scholasticism and the spiritual oppression by the Moscovite orthodoxy."

⁶ The same author stressed even more clearly Skovoroda's love for Sacred Scripture in: Ivan Mirtschuk, **Geschichte der ukrainischen Kultur** (München, 1957) 124: "Skovoroda interessierte sich lebhaft für religiöse Fragen, teilweise deshalb, weil er auf diese Art der Überlieferung seiner Hochschule treu blieb, und teilweise auch aus dem Grunde, da diese Fragen die damalige ukrainische Gesellschaft in hohem Masse beschäftigten. Dieser Vorliebe entsprang auch sein Studium der Bibel, 'des weisesten aller Bücher, das seinen langjährigen Hunger und Durst mit der göttlichen Wahrheit stillte'. Gut vertraut mit dem theologischen Schrifttum versuchte er, den Text der Bibel mit Hilfe eines von ihm zusammengestellten Schlüssels von Symbolen zu erklären."

⁷ The First Vatican Council considered and defined these matters in a Dogmatic Constitution, **De Fide Catholica "Dei Filius",** which was promulgated during the third session (April 24, 1870); cf. H. Denzinger and A. Schönmetzer, **Enchiridion Symbolorum...** (Barcinonae etc., 1963³²) 3000-3045. The Second Vatican Council developed these questions further in a Dogmatic Constitution, **De divina Revelatione "Dei Verbum",** (November 18, 1965).

⁸ For more exact information see: K. Rahner and H. Vorgrimler, "Philosophie und Theologie", in: **Kleines theologisches Wörterbuch** (Freiburg i. Br., 1963) 287-289; G. F. Van Ackeren, "Reflections on the Relation between Philosophy and Theology", in: **Theological Studies** 14 (1953) 527-550.

⁹ Hryhorij Skovoroda, **Tvory v dvoch tomach** (Kyjiv, 1961) 1, 16 ("Nachalnaja dver ko khrystianskomu dobronraviju").

¹⁰ **Ibidem** 1, 84 ("Symfonia, narechennaja knyha Askhanj, o poznaniji samaho sebe").

¹¹ **Ibidem** 1, 188 ("Dialoh, ili razhalahol o drevnem mirje").

¹² **Ibidem** 1, 320 ("Razhovor, nazyvaemyj alfavit, ili bukvar mira"). The author signed the preface of this work: "Lubytel svjaschennyja Bibliji, Hryhorij Skovoroda" [-"Lover of the sacred Bible, Hryhorij Skovoroda"].

¹³ **Ibidem** 1, 377-8 ("Knyžechka, nazyvajemaja Silenus Alcibiadis, syrjech ikona alkiviadskaja [Izrailskij zmij]").

¹⁴ **Ibidem** 1, 439 ("Branj arkhistratyha Mikhajila so Satanoju o sem: lehko bytj blahym").

¹⁵ **Ibidem** 1, 491 ("Blahorodnyj Erodij").

¹⁶ **Ibidem** 1, 515 ("Ubohyj žajvoronok. Prytcha").

¹⁷ **Ibidem** 1, 470 ("Prja Bisu so Varcaboju").

¹⁸ **Ibidem** II, 5-57.

¹⁹ **Ibidem** II, 47.

²⁰ **Ibidem** I, 352.

²¹ **Ibidem** II, 101-150.

²² **Ibidem** II, 102-103: "The very sum of all the planets and the empress Bible was created by God from figures representing the mysteries, from parables, and from similes. The whole was fashioned from clay, and is called in [St.] Paul, ignorance. However, the spirit of life was breathed into this clay, and in this ignorance the wisdom of all mortal things lieth hidden."

²³ **Ibidem** II, 145-150. There we find fourteen biblical quotations.

²⁴ **Ibidem** I, 17.

²⁵ **Ibidem** I, 24.

²⁶ **Ibidem** I, 26.

²⁷ Cf. note 1.

²⁸ Hryhorij Skovoroda, **Tvory v dvoch tomach** (Kyjiv, 1961) I, 14.

²⁹ **Ibidem** I, 42.

³⁰ On the concept of "heart" in the Bible and theology see: P. Hoffmann and K. Rahner, "Herz", in: **Handbuch theologisher Grundbegriffe,** ed. H. Fries (München, 1962) I, 687-697; O. Schroeder, N. Adler, and A. Maxein, "Herz", in **LThK,**² V, 285-287; W. E. Lynch, "Heart (in the Bible)", in: **New Catholic Encyclopedia** (New York etc., 1967) VI, 965.

the
UKRAINIAN CATHOLIC
LAY MOVEMENT
1945-1975.
AN INTERPRETATION

Originally published in *The Ukrainian Catholic Church 1945-1975. A Symposium.*
Miroslav Labunka and Leonid Rudnytzky, editors (Philadelphia: The St.Sophia Religious Association of Ukrainian Catholics, Inc., 1976), pp. 90−106. Reprinted here with permission.

THE UKRAINIAN CATHOLIC LAY
MOVEMENT 1945-1975:
AN INTERPRETATION

Petro B. T. Bilaniuk

In addressing a group of Ukrainians, Father George Maloney, S.J., once said the following words:

> You too must come to know who you are. You must know the family you came from with all its history. And how little we really know about the Ukrainian nation.[1]

I

In order to respond to this challenging statement and to grasp at least superficially the inner condition of the Ukrainian Catholic Church in the diaspora, and understand the activity and mentality of its hierarchy, as well as the ethos of its lay movement, it is necessary to analyze the Ukrainian psyche and the religiosity which emanates from it. Thus we must discuss some aspects of *ethnopsychology* of the Ukrainian nation.

Ethnopsychology is understood here as a branch of science investigating the psyche or a psychological set-up and distinctive characteristics of a particular people or nation with all of its constituent elements, aspects or factors, i.e., psychosomatic (racial), geographical (geophysic), historical, psychosocial, cultural (including religion and religiosity), and psychoanalytical.[2]

The term *nation* as used in this paper is not synonymous with the American usage of the term. It should not be understood here as a body of inhabitants of a country united under a single independent government, i.e. a state. The term is used here to denote a biological and cultural entity characterized by ties of blood, by a common language, culture, religion, tradition, customs, art as well as by a consciousness of a socio-cultural homogeneity; a people with a collective will, common memory, mutual interest, and future goals.[3]

The ethnopsychology of the Ukrainian nation[4] reveals to us that the Ukrainian psyche was formed and determined by four principle frontiers: geographical, geopolitical, philosophical and spiritual. Geographically, Ukraine is located on the Eastern frontier of Europe. Therefore, it comprises both geographically and culturally a transitional situation between East and West. The rich Ukrainian soil, the natural beauty of the country and its moderate climate made Ukraine a very coveted country by all its neighbors. Both trade and cultural routes crossed in Ukraine leaving upon it a distinctive cosmopolitan imprint.

On the other hand, this geopolitical situation was a constant invitation to innumerable invasions by Asiatic hordes as well as by other neighbors, who brought with them destruction, suffering, plagues, hunger, and death. This state of affairs had a very profound influence upon the spiritual formation of the Ukrainian people; it placed them in an existential frontier situation between life and death, existence and non-existence. This in turn precipitated inner psychological crises and imposed a profound sapiential reflection about the meaning of existence which resulted in uncertitude, anxiety, pessimism, and melancholic resignation.

Throughout the centuries, the chivalrous type of Ukrainian man took up the sword and defended his native land from hostile invaders. Since the odds were usually against the defending force, the number of defenders constantly diminished, for they died on the battlefield and left reproduction to the cautious peasant, who evaded battles in order to stay alive. Thus there was a constant diminishing of the heroic type of life and a constant increase of a private and withdrawn type of existence of the peasant who feels responsibility only for his immediate surroundings.

The central problem of the Ukrainian spiritual make-up is the co-existence of two contrasting elements: the heroic, chivalrous (or simply Cossack) ideal of life and the withdrawn, passive, private and asocial existence of the peasant. The heroic ideal lives on in songs, rites, folklore, preaching and in the very intense historic memory of the Ukrainian nation. Everybody looks up to this ideal, and yet it remains an unattainable good. This, in turn, results in a profound introversion, guilt complex and unrealistic dreams of glory.[5] In order to compensate for their failure and to rid themselves of the guilt complex, Ukrainians are unique as a nation in celebrating major military defeats as national feast days, e.g., Kruty, Bazar, Brody,* paying tribute to their dead heroes not because they gained anything for Ukraine (except glory) but because they

---

*These are the names of the three towns in Ukraine where Ukrainians suffered defeats at the hands of the Soviet Russian armed forces in 1918, 1921, and 1944 respectively.

correspond to the heroic ideal which the majority of Ukrainians is not capable of achieving.

Nevertheless, there are also positive sides to the Ukrainian psyche. In spite of catastrophes and disasters which the Ukrainian nation has had to suffer and which it has successfully survived, Ukrainians have developed some positive characteristics, i.e., attitudes, which do not directly seek socio-political or economic expansion, but which strive toward moral values, which make up the meaning of the "Ukrainian glory," i.e., a sapiential type of synthesis of goodness, beauty, truth, justice and love. This is the optimistic side of the Ukrainian national psyche, the source of its incredible resistance and persistence and which has helped the Ukrainian nation to survive centuries of adverse conditions.

The most negative trait of the Ukrainian psyche, however, is an exaggerated individualism which, if kept in check, is a sign of the unity of the Ukrainian nation with Western European individualism. In its exaggerated form it leads to the abyss of anarchy. Thus we can conclude with Wolodymyr Janiw that:

> Basically the reasons for our historical calamities, inasmuch as they emerged from an exaggerated Ukrainian individualism, can be characterized by a paradox: we landed in subjugation, because we have an excessive love of freedom. In desiring equality and brotherhood we were afraid of our own despot and weakened ourselves by internal strife, until aliens began to dominate us.[6]

Furthermore, under foreign domination, where free self-expression is impossible, the spirit of resistance to and hatred of the alien yoke quite naturally gives rise to an inner negative attitude of rejecting any authority, anarchical outbursts, lack of discipline, and a generally negative attitude towards life. The Ukrainian people are thus inwardly torn between a desire for freedom and a desire for a strong personality, who would reunite and lead the nation to statehood and the Church to autonomy in the Ukrainian Patriarchate. Thus two tendencies of the unbalanced Ukrainian psyche are destroying each other: the disposition to self-expression and autonomy constantly revolts against the necessity to submit to the legitimate authority and to cooperate with it.

On the other hand Ukrainians in authority, beset by an inferiority complex, often compensate by tyrannical tendencies and attitudes, which recall those of their foreign overlords, thus destroying confidence and making the authority in question ineffective and prone to be rejected by their compatriots. Some attitudes of this kind are: demands for instant obedience, refusal to listen to other ideas, a tendency to answer criticism with insults, and an inability to respect a dissenting position and still lead effectively.

Without exception all investigators of the ethnopsychic make-up of the Ukrainian nation have arrived at the conclusion that Ukrainians are a highly emotional people. In their lives emotions play such an important role that they dominate or even overshadow the functioning of the intellect and will. This expresses itself in emotionalism, sentimentality, delicacy of feelings and lyricism, and more concretely in the aestheticism of the Ukrainian folklore, ritualism, embroideries, music, and songs. This emotionalism creates an aura of a profound introversion which, in combination with a relatively weak intellect and will, explains why Ukrainians very easily display incredible enthusiasm and cool down even more quickly. This in turn explains why Ukrainians are excited by relatively unimportant details and remain passive when confronted by important matters which overwhelm them and which, in many instances, they are unable to comprehend.[8]

Many of us have witnessed and participated in what appeared to be rallies on national and ecclesial feastdays which seemed to signify a great awakening, the beginning of a new era and of a new movement. And yet, they passed without a trace, except for the emotional remorse of being unable to continue this trend. This temporary megalomania is actually an artificially created state of mind, a pretense of power and unity to compensate for the deep-rooted inferiority complex resulting from a long stateless existence.

II

The above definitions of ethnopsychology and nation, as well as the observations of the ethnopsychological peculiarities of the Ukrainians, are important for the correct understanding of the Ukrainian Catholic Church. The Ukrainian Catholic Church, like most of the Eastern Churches, is a national Church in which these specific Ukrainian ethnopsychological peculiarities are clearly manifested. For example, whenever a Ukrainian Catholic speaks of a "patriarch," he has simultaneously in mind an "ethnarch," a religious leader who is the father of the nation and at the same time its chief representative on the international scene. Many Ukrainians accord priority to the idea of ethnarch over the idea of patriarch, although they may not even be aware of the term "ethnarch".[9] The same can be said of an Eastern Christian idea of patriarchate or of a particular and autonomous church. In the Christian East these are understood quite rightly not as exclusively religious institutions, but as properties of each particular Christian nation in which the entire national patrimony lives and is handed down from generation to generation as a sacred, religious and national good. Thus the Western type of separation of Church and state is alien to the mind of Eastern Christians in general and to the Ukrainian mind in particular because the stress is placed on a different plane, namely on the Church-nation relationship. It is understood that should a free and independent Ukrainian state emerge, there will be a very intimate cooperation between Church and state, just as there is now a very close bond between Church and nation.

This religious (or rather ecclesiological) ideology produces among Ukrainians a nostalgic desire for "One Nation - One Church" which found its strongest expression in a booklet with a homonymous title by M. Bradovych.[10] Understanding of these interrelationships is important for non-Ukrainians, for they explain why there is a lack of ecumenical dialogue and cooperation between different Ukrainian ecclesial groups, i.e., Orthodox, Catholic, and Protestant. Each of the Churches desires to be the only true Ukrainian Church which would reunite under its auspices all Ukrainians. This is also the reason why my proposal and terminology of the three branches of the one Ukrainian Church, viz., Orthodox, Catholic, and Protestant,[11] was in fact rejected by the representatives of the Ukrainian Orthodox and Catholic branches even if it did find some resonance among the people at large. It was accepted by the Ukrainian Protestants, who are desperately trying to prove that they are not a "foreign import" into the Ukrainian community and that they constitute an integral part of Ukrainian ecclesial reality. In other words, the idea of religious pluralism is extremely weak among Ukrainians, for most of them seem to be persuaded that there must be one nation, one Church, one denomination, one civil and one religious government.

For many centuries Ukrainians made up an agricultural society of peasants; they constituted practically a one-class nation. The uper classes were usually foreign overlords. As recently as in 1926, 92% of all Ukrainians in Ukraine and in the diaspora were peasants. Therefore, a very typical ethnopsychological trait of the Ukrainian nation is its spiritual bond with the soil, which in the Ukrainian mind assumed mythical and mystical dimensions and became a lengendary entity with secret and life-giving powers. Ukrainians were always sensitive to the processes of nature. They perceived very strongly nature's goodness, its fruitfulness and graciousness, which they interpreted in the moral and mystical dimension as the bestowing love, with which such phenomena as the fruitful soil, the golden sun, the friendly breeze, and light rain cooperate. Therefore Ukrainians as an agricultural nation developed a very strong cosmic religious sense, which in theological terminology is described as panentheism, that is, an intense presence and immanence of God in His creatures.[12]

Ukrainian religiosity is not based on the *phobos*-type of religion; it is not based on fear. It is partially an *eros*-type of religion, in the center of which stands the archetype of mother with all her female and motherly qualities and characteristics: goodness, economic sense, and an intense love of children for whom it is necessary to preserve the fruits of the soil. Thus the native soil is called the Great Mother who among other things is a remnant of primitive Indo-Germanic religion.[13] This *eros*-type of religion among Ukrainians is closely connected with the *agape*-type of religion, based on mutual and social love. The consequences of this has been a very great prominence of the mother in social life, which very often bordered on a matriarchal system of society. This also explains why Mariology and Marian devotion in Ukraine reached their pinnacle and are unsurpassed in the whole world.

Among Ukrainians the *nomos*-type of religion is relatively little developed. There are few laws, few good lawyers and canonists, few philosophical and speculative minds. Therefore any written agreement or concordat in Ukrainian history or church-life have been typically poorly worded and usually have been abused by unscrupulous non-Ukrainian parties. A further consequence of a certain lack of *nomos*-type of religion among Ukrainians is the confusion of wishful thinking and actual rights which must be defended and used. From this originates a lack of analysis of history and Church-history in particular, a lack of understanding of diplomacy and its intricacies and a naive acceptance of the statements of others at face value. Usually there is a lack of long-range planning and an inability to foresee the consequences of certain actions and events.

III

The above theoretical ethnopsychological and ethnoreligious considerations will help us to interpret the Ukrainian lay movement since 1945. At the end of World War II many Ukrainians found themselves in Western Europe, especially in Germany, Austria, and Italy, but also in Great Britain, France, and Belgium. During this period several religiously oriented organizations emerged which continued the tradition of the organized laity in Ukraine. These were Catholic Action;[14] *Obnova* - Ukrainian Catholic Students' Organization, which was part of the International Catholic Students' Organization, *Pax Romana; Mariis'ka Druzhyna*, (the Sodality of Our Lady) belonging to the Roman *Prima Primaria*; and many other local organizations, like the Brotherhood of Prayer and Church Brotherhoods and Sisterhoods.

All these organizations had several things in common: they were created and fully controlled by the hierarchy, at that time the Apostolic Visitor for Ukrainians in Western Europe, Archbishop Ivan Buchko (1891-1974) in Rome, his vicars general in different countries, and local priests. This was during the pontificate of

Pius XII (1939-1958), a stout anticommunist, a great friend of all suffering Churches, and especially of the Ukrainian Catholic Church as expressed in his encyclical *Orientales omnes ecclesias,* dated December 23, 1945, which was totally dedicated to the history and contemporary condition of the Ukrainian Catholic Church. Thus the Ukrainian Catholic Church in the diaspora and especially in Western Europe felt quite secure and did not anticipate any change of policy by the Holy Roman Apostolic See. At that time the Congregation for the Eastern Churches was headed by the Pope himself in the capacity of prefect. The Secretariate of the Congregation rested in the hands of His Eminence Eugene Cardinal Tisserant (a great friend of the Eastern Churches in general and of the Ukrainian Catholic Church in particular despite his strong Russophile tendencies). In the long history of the relations of the Apostolic Roman See with the Eastern Churches, Cardinal Tisserant played a very important role. He worked hard to de-Latinize the Eastern Churches, especially in liturgical matters. Under his guidance the Roman See started to issue liturgical books. A rule *(Ordo celebrationis)* how to celebrate liturgical functions was also issued (Rome, 1944). Incredibly enough both the clergy and in many instances the laity resented these "innovations" and clung tenaciously to their Latinized form of worship, structure of Church organizations, and to a Western type of spirituality. This situation can be explained in the following way: Pope Pius XII represented to the Ukrainians the figure of a good father who was taking care of his Ukrainian children, especially of the Ukrainian theological students in the Pontifical Ukrainian College of St. Josaphat in Rome, the Ukrainian lay students at the University of Louvain for whom a special Ukrainian house was established, the Ukrainian scholarly center of the Shevchenko Scientific Society in Sarcelles, France, etc. As pointed out above, the Ukrainian Catholic community in Europe was fully satisfied with their "Mother Church," with the exception of the "liturgical innovations" which were usually interpreted as an attempt to conform the Ukrainian Catholic Church to the Russian liturgical tradition.

We can safely say that generally speaking this period of time was not very conducive to the further development of the Ukrainian Catholic Church. The Ukrainian laity and clergy did not manage to delve into deeper study and rediscovery of their rich, profound Eastern Christian heritage. They were overwhelmed by the Roman Church and in their inferiority complex looked up to the Latin rite, Latin ecclesiastical tradition, and centralism.

The Ukrainian Catholic lay organizations which have been mentioned performed positive socio-political and ecclesial functions. They organized many important rallies in defense of the Ukrainian Catholic Church in the catacombs and informed the world about this by special publications as well as through the international press.[15]

The situation started to change very rapidly in the late forties and early fifties when the major bulk of Ukrainians emigrated to the USA, Canada, Australia, and the countries of Latin America. In the countries of their new settlement they found church-sponsored organizations of Ukrainian laity which were organized on the parish and exarchate levels. In Canada they found and joined the Ukrainian Catholic Brotherhood in Canada *(BUKK)*, the Ukrainian Catholic Women's League, Ukrainian Catholic Youth, the Ukrainian Mutual Benefit Association of St. Nicholas (also called St. Nicholas Brotherhood) of Canada, the Knights of Columbus of St. Josaphat, and many others.[16] In the USA they found and joined "the Apostleship of Prayer, Sodality, Children of Mary, Holy Name Society, Knights of Columbus councils, Ukrainian Catholic Youth League and Altar Boy Society . . . fraternal-benevolent societies, the Providence Association with its publication *America*."[17]

These Church organizations of the laity were even less in the line of tradition of Ukrainian Brotherhoods and Sisterhoods which existed in Ukraine throughout history.[18] Their statutes and rules stipulate to the present day that the so-called "spiritual assistant," always a bishop or priest, can veto any decision of the chapter entrusted to him, or of the eparchial or national executive.[19] Therefore these organizations rarely ventured beyond purely auxiliary duties in the parish churches, such as the collection of money and the organization of banquets and feast-days. Sometimes they organized retreats or lectures which rarely went beyond the level of catechism. Therefore, when the Second Vatican Council came into session, and especially when His Beatitude the Metropolitan of Halych, Archbishop of L'viv and Bishop of Kamianets' Podils'kyi, Josyf Slipyj was released from his imprisonment in Siberia and the struggle for Ukrainian Patriarchate and Church autonomy became acute, these organizations not only were not prepared for these tasks, but on the contrary, assumed a negative stance or lapsed into total passivity.

By 1955 the resettlement of Ukrainians from Europe to the Americas and Australia was over. It was necessary to reorganize the Ukrainian diaspora in Europe, which by now was relatively small. Under the dynamic leadership of Professor Wolodymyr Janiw there came into being in 1953 the *Ukrainian Christian Movement*, which encompassed most of the European countries in which Ukrainians lived. This organization merits special attention for it exists to the present day as an ecumenically structured entity consisting of Catholic and Orthodox branches, which cooperate very closely with each other. Further, this organization was able to establish very good contacts with Latin rite Catholic organizations in different countries of Western Europe and to participate in world congresses of the Catholic laity. It served all classes of the Ukrainian diaspora by organizing pilgrimages, feastdays, lectures, etc., and by its publications. The latter merit special consideration; the Ukrainian Christian Movement has published a volume of essays entitled *Ukrainian Laymen in the Life of the Church, the Society and Mankind*.[20] In this volume 17 authors try to give a scholarly assessment of the rights, possibilities, and obligations of the Ukrainian laity in the changing conditions of the modern world. Unfortunately this volume has not received the attention it deserves. However, the Ukrainian Christian Movement was unable to establish itself in the New World and to compete with existing lay organizations. Nor did it participate fully in the struggle for the establishment of the Ukrainian Patriarchate.

IV

The year 1964 marked the promulgation of the *Decree on the Eastern Catholic Churches* by Vatican II and the emergence of several groups in Toronto, Chicago, and Cleveland, which called themselves Committees for the Defense of Rite and Tradition of the Ukrainian Catholic Church, or used similar names. This was the beginning of the protest movement against the Latinization and assimilation of the Ukrainian Catholic Church in Canada and the United States of America, perpetrated by the Ukrainian Catholic hierarchy, under pressure from the Roman Curia and the representatives of the Latin hierarchies of these countries. The situation had changed completely since 1959 when Cardinal Tisserant was recalled from the office of the Secretary of the Congregation for the Eastern Churches — the prelates who succeeded him in that office reflected the renewed trend of Latinization and assimilation of the Eastern Catholic Churches in general, and of the Ukrainian Catholic Church in particular. These same people wanted to sabotage the *Decree on the Eastern Catholic Churches* even before its official promulgation (e.g. Maximilian Cardinal de Fuerstenberg).

The issues in question which were raised by the Committees mentioned above were the forceful introduction of the Gregorian calendar, Latinization of liturgical practices, church art and architecture, the prohibition against ordaining married candidates to the priesthood and the realization of the autonomy of the Eastern Catholic Churches as reaffirmed by Vatican II.

These Defense Committees, as they became known in abbreviated form, were trying to fight a double battle; on the parish and eparchial levels they tried to defend the spiritual heritage of the

Ukrainian Church, its rights, tradition, and language while at the same time they tried to support the movement for the establishment of the Ukrainian Patriarchate of Kyiv and Halych. In addition, they tried to realize in practice the personal jurisdiction of the head of the Ukrainian Catholic Church over all members of that Church, including metropolitans, archbishops, bishops, clergy, all monastic orders, and the laity throughout the world, who belonged to Byzantine-Ukrainian (Greek-Ruthenian) Rite. The Committee of Defense in Toronto scored a first by initiating a religious type of publication without the *imprimatur* of the Church authorities. This was a little pamphlet in Ukrainian by Reverend Clayton Barclay entitled *A Foreigner in the Defense of the Ukrainian Church* (Toronto, 1966).[21] This was followed by my pamphlet in Ukrainian entitled *The Ukrainian Church — Its Present and Future* (Toronto — Chicago, 1966). Finally in July of 1966, there appeared the first issue of the bulletin *Za ridnu Tserkvu (For Our Native Church)* which appears irregularly to the present day.

In December 1966, all existing committees held their first Congress in Chicago, Illinois, and created the Central Committee for the Defense of Rite, Tradition and Language of the Ukrainian Catholic Church in USA and Canada.[22] This strengthened the defensive front and soon the hierarchy was obliged to revise many of its positions. However, for quite a while the work of the Committee in Toronto was paralyzed by an internal division into two warring factions, which greatly decreased the effectiveness of its work.

In 1965, there emerged in the United States the Society for the Promotion of the Patriarchal System in the Ukrainian Catholic Church, the members of which became known as *patriiarkhal'nyky*. This Society exhibited tremendous dynamism and soon numbered 17 chapters, scattered all over the United States with many representatives in smaller localities. In 1967, the Society started to publish its bulletin *Za Patriiarkhat (For the Patriarchate)*, which over the years assembled a tremendous wealth of material and informed the Ukrainian and later, through its English pages, the non-Ukrainian audience as well.[23]

At the suggestion of Major Archbishop and Cardinal Josyf Slipyj there came into being in July of 1969 the World Association for the Erection of the Patriarchate of the Ukrainian Catholic Church. This central organization soon was able to establish national executives in those countries of the world with Ukrainian settlements, such as Argentina, Belgium, England, France, Germany, Spain, and Venezuela. Two representatives from Australia were appointed to work with the World Association.[24]

Tensions arose between the World Association and the National Executive of the Society for the Promotion of the Patriarchal System in the Ukrainian Catholic Church in the USA which were never satisfactorily resolved until the dissolution of the World Federation on December 29, 1974 in Washington, when the Ukrainian Patriarchal World Federation came into being, which united all Ukrainian lay organizations and committees as well as some church-sponsored organizations of laity. In the meantime, a conference held in Toronto on March 7-8, 1970, created by a rather undemocratic procedure the Coordinating Committee of the Ukrainian Organizations in Canada and USA for the Realization of the Patriarchate of the Ukrainian Catholic Church.[25] This new umbrella organization coordinated different religious and civic Ukrainian organizations which had expressed a willingness to participate in the struggle for the establishment of the Ukrainian Patriarchate and for strengthening the autonomy of the Particular Ukrainian Catholic Church. In major centers of Ukrainian settlement, local councils of these organizations emerged which organized petitions to the Pope and the Roman Curia as well as rallies and festivities in honor of His Beatitude Major Archbishop Josyf Slipyj, or in honor of the Particular and Patriarchal Ukrainian Catholic Church.

All these organizations and bodies of organizations had several things in common. There was a definite lack of necessary contact with the lay movements and organizations of other autonomous and local churches in the Catholic Church including organizations of Latin rite laity. In spite of assurances that they act independently and on their own initiative, these organizations soon became dominated by the hierarchy, for in many instances they did not know what steps to take. Thus the painful lack of theologically, canonically, and historically trained laity became apparent. In many instances these organizations did not cooperate with their local hierarchy, but established contacts with members of the hierarchy in a different country of Ukrainian settlement, preferably beyond the ocean, on the assumption that this distant hierarchy was better than their immediate ecclesiastical superiors. Little did they realize that all members of the Ukrainian Catholic hierarchy were equally intimidated by the Roman Curia and were unwilling to jeopardize their positions. The leaders of these organizations lacked knowledge of Church history in general and of Ukrainian Church history in particular. Therefore they were prone to take documents and statements emanating from the Pope, the Roman Curia, or the Ukrainian Catholic hierarchy at face value. They had no diplomatic skill and no understanding of the operations of Vatican diplomacy. As a result there were usually no preliminaries through contacts with intermediaries but always a direct and open frontal attack of the problem, e.g., writing of petitions directly to the top authority — the Pope — without even ensuring that he would get their message or that he would be influenced by his advisors to take them seriously into consideration. All this became quite evident during the furor which was raised by the letter of Cardinal Tisserant in which he succinctly stated the position of the Vatican and not his own as regards the dignity of the Patriarchate of Moscow and its Russian possessors and the relative unimportance or even non-existence of Ukrainians and their Church.[26]

A detailed analysis of the activities of the Ukrainian Catholic lay organizations reveals a definite pattern:

1. A spectacular beginning with an overloaded and unrealistic program.

2. A short period of rest during which the unrealistic nature of the program became apparent and the first signs of rivalries appeared, which grew until the end of an organization.

3. Petitions to the Pope, resolutions, and letters full of emotionalism, written either in a subservient tone or containing the kind of strongly worded statements which people are prone to make when they are offended. Most of the time these letters remain unanswered. This in turn aggravates the inferiority complex and increases the rivalries and disputes.

4. Having written petitions and letters, the executive of a certain organization convened rallies and in highly pitched tones informed the audience of its achievements, promising an even brighter and more glorious future.

5. Next followed different types of publications, including materials gathered from the four previous activities described above, apologies of the executive and attacks against enemies and incompetent persons from within and without the Ukrainian Catholic Church.

6. Having exhausted all their inner energy, organizations entered a period of disenchantment, divisions, and a slow lapse into oblivion or an act of self-liquidation.

V

From the ethnopsychological point of view the Ukrainian lay organizations founded and dominated by the hierarchy represent the passive, quiet, cautious, and matriarchal segment of the Ukrainian Church and nation. Their members are concerned with the immediate problems of their parish and their horizon usually ends at the level of their own eparchy.

Lay organizations founded by the laity, on the other hand, resemble the hero-type of Ukrainian, who in decisive moments gathers his inner energy and reacts with vehemence and extroversion seeking glory first of all and freedom, independence, and other human values. Their life is short and intense. They seek to transform the Ukrainian Church and Ukrainian nation from a matriarchal type of society and from divided fiefdoms ruled by aristocracy into a strongly centralized patriarchal type of society, operated monarchically from above. They seem to believe that a patriarch will be able to solve all the problems in a church which from a closed society in Galicia (Western Ukraine) has become a worldwide empire,while trying desperately to preserve its identity and connection with the Mother Church in Ukraine. This, obviously, is an illusion, for while the establishment of the Patriarchate would be a tremendous step forward and a great help in the struggle of the Ukrainian Catholic Church to preserve its identity, success can be attained only as the result of a regeneration of the whole Ukrainian Catholic Church in all its aspects and dimensions. This is an extremely complex process which demands tremendous and continuous effort and the cooperation of the hierarchy, clergy, and laity. For the time being neither segment of the Ukrainian Catholic Church seems to be ready for this task.

---

[1]G. Maloney, *What Does it Mean to be a Ukrainian Catholic? And Ukrainian Catholic Autonomy* (Weston, Ont., St. Demetrius Ukrainian Catholic Church [1975]), p. 19.

[2]The division proposed here is adapted from A. Kultschytsky (O. Kul'chyts'kyi), "National Characteristics of the Ukrainian People", *Ukraine: A Concise Encyclopaedia*, vol. I ([Toronto, 1963]), pp. 946-953. Ethnopsychology became an independent discipline with the publication of the *Zeitschrift für Völkerpsychologie und Sprachwissenschaft* (Bd. 1-20, edited by M. Lazarus, H. Steinthal, and others, 1860-1890, in Berlin and, for a short period of time, in Leipzig. Afterwards it was continued as: *Zeitshrift des Vereins für Volkskunde.*).

[3]On the origin, formation, and the nature of the Ukrainian nation, cf.: V. Pachovs'kyi, *Ukraintsi iak narid* (Chernivtsi, 1907?); B. Ol'khivs'kyi, *Vil'nyi narid* (Warsaw, 1938); V. Shcherbakivs'kyi, *Formatsiia ukrains'koi natsii* (Prague, 1941); D. Dontsov, *Dukh nashoi davnyny* (Prague, 1944; 2nd abbr. ed., Regensburg, 1951); V. Petrov, *Pokhodzhennia ukrains'koho narodu* (Regensburg, 1947); Iu. Rusov, *Dusha narodu i dukh natsii* (Philadelphia, 1948); and L. Rebet, *Formuvannia ukrains'koi natsii* (Munich, 1951).

[4]On ethnopsychology of the Ukrainian nation — in addition to the works listed in footnote no. 3, cf.: N. Kostomarov, "Dve russkie narodnosti", *Osnova*, 1861 (St. Petersburg), no. 3; I. Nechui - Levyts'kyi, *Svitohliad ukrains'koho narodu* (L'viv, 1878); V. Antonovych, "Try natsional'ni typy", *Pravda*, 1888 (L'viv); T. R[yl'skii], "K izucheniiu ukrainskago narodnago mirovozzreniia", *Kievskaia starina*, 1888 (Kiev), no. 11; 1890, nos. 9-10; 1905, nos. 4-5; L. Tsehel's'kyi, *Rus'-Ukraina i*

Moskovshchyna (L'viv, 1900); *idem, Rus'-Ukraina i Moskovshchyna-Rosiia* (Constantinople, 1915); V. Sikorskii, *Vseobshchaia psikhologiia s fiziognomikoi* (Kiev, 1912); I. Ohiienko, *Istoriia ukrains'koi kul'tury* (Kamianets' Podil's'kyi, 1920); V. Lypyns'kyi, *Lysty do brativ-khliborobiv . . .* (Vienna, 1926; Kh. Vovk, *Studii z ukrains'koi etnohrafii ta antropolohii* (Prague, 1927); D. Chyzhevs'kyi, *Narysy z istorii filosofii na Ukraini* (Prague, 1931); *idem,* "Holovni rysy ukrains'-koho svitohliadu", in: *Ukrains'ka kul'tura* (Podebrady, 1940); R. Iendyk, *Antropolohichni prykmety ukrains'koho narodu* (L'viv, 1934); I. Mirtschuk (I. Mirchuk):1) "Die slavische Philosophie in ihren Grundzügen und Hauptproblemen", *Kyrios,* Bd. 2 (Königsberg, 1936), pp. 157-175; 2) "Die geistigen Merkmale des ukrainischen Volkes", in: *Handbuch der Ukraine* (Leipzig, 1941), pp. 74-83 (Published also in English: "The Basic Traits of the Ukrainian People," in: *Ukraine and its People* (Munich, 1949), pp. 35-54; 3) *Das Dämonishe bei den Russen und Ukrainern)* (Augsburg, 1950) (Ukrains'ka Vil'na Akademiia Nauk, VIII); 4) *Geschichte der ukrainischen Kultur* (Munich, [1957]), pp. 55-69, 256-257. (*Veröffentlichungen* des Osteuropa-Institutes München, Bd. 12); I. Krypiakevych, *Istoriia ukrains'koi kul'tury* (L'viv, 1937); Iu. Lypa, *Pryznachennia Ukrainy* (L'viv, 1937; reprinted in New York, 1953); P. Fedenko, "Vplyv istorii na ukrains'kyi narodnii kharakter", *Naukovyi zbirnyk UVU,* III (Prague, 1942); *idem,* "Svitohliad ukrains'koho narodu", *ibidem;* A. Brückner, *Dzieje kultury polskiej,* t. I-IV (Cracow, 1946); O. Kul'chyts'kyi, "Rysy kharakterolohii ukrains'koho narodu", in: *Entsyklopediia ukrainoznavstva,* t. 1/II (Munich, 1949), pp. 708-718; M. Shlemkevych, ed., *Ukrains'ka dusha* (New York, 1956). It includes contributions by the following authors: Ie. Onats'kyi, "Ukrains'ka emotsiinist' ", pp. 5-12; O. Kul'chyts'kyi, "Svitovidchuvannia ukraintsia", pp. 13-25; B. Tsymbalistyi, "Rodyna i dusha narodu", pp. 26-43; and M. Shlemkevych, "Dusha i pisnia", pp. 44-54; V. Ianiv (V. Janiw) "Ukrains'ka vdacha i nash vykhovnyi ideal", in: *Pedahohichni problemy ta dydaktychni porady* (Munich, 1969), pp. 1-17; and *idem,* "Do systematyzatsii pohliadiv Ivana Mirchuka na ukrains'ku liudynu", in: *Zbirnyk na poshanu Ivana Mirchuka. Symbolae in memoriam Ioannis Mirtschuk* (1891-1961), *A. v. Kultschytzkyj,* ed. (Munich et. al., 1974), pp. 149-194 (Bibliography) (Universitas Libera Ucrainensis, *Studia,* t. VIII).

[5]A. H. Velykyi ("Relihiia i Tserkva — osnovni rushii ukrains'koi istorii", in: V. Ianiv, ed., *Relihiia v zhytti ukrains'koho narodu* (Munich-Rome,Paris, 1966), pp. 3-38), is right when he observes that "glory" (*slava*) is the true catalyst of and the key to the Ukrainian history. For him glory is goodness and beauty in all their humanistic broadness, accepted and recognized as such. In support of this view, the author adduces very interesting arguments, one of which is most significant. In 250 years of Ukrainian history (X-XIII centuries) the names of more than 120 Ukrainian princes and 27 princesses contain the word *slava* or its variants in various combinations, e.g. Boles*lav,* Briachys*lav,* Vyshes*lav,* Iaros*lav.* Comp. also G. P. Fedotov, *The Russian Religious Mind,* vol. I. *Kievan Christianity: The Tenth to the Thirteenth Centuries* (Cambridge, Mass., MCMLXVI. Available also as a *Harper Torchbooks,* TB 70, ed., New York, 1960), pp. 329-333.

[6]V. Ianiv, "Ukrains'ka vdacha i nash vykhovnyi ideal," pp. 6-7.

[7]It would be to the benefit of Ukrainian leaders, both civic and ecclesiastical, to examine the ideas set forth in: *Problems of Authority*, ed. by J. M. Todd (Baltimore-London, 1962).

[8]I. Mirtschuk (*Geschichte der ukrainischen Kultur*, pp. 64-65), for example, makes the following observations about the Ukrainian mentality: "Keine übermassige Systematik, sondern eher Systemlosigkeit, dafür aber oft geniale Intuition, die unbewusst und aus dem Gefühl heraus ihre Konstruktionen schafft. Keine Gründlichkeit, keine Vertiefung mit zwangsläufiger Einschränkung des Tätigkeitsgebietes, sondern im Gegenteil eine viel zu starke Erweiterung der Interessensphäre mit gleichzeitiger Verflachung der Arbeit. Keine vernunftgemässe begriffliche Behandlung der Probleme in Theorie und Praxis, sodern gefühlsmässige Erfassung der Wirklichkeit, Unmittelbarkeit des Entschlusses aus dem Affekt heraus und endlich die Vermengung der theoretischen und praktischen Momente . . . Da alle drei Funktionen: Verstand, Gefühl und Wille in enger Abhängigkeit voneinander stehen, wird die Vorherrschaft der ersten oder der zweiten auch die Tätigkeit der dritten notwendigerweise beeinflussen. Das vom Gefühl und nicht vom Verstand beherrschte Wollen wird keinesfalls grosse Festigkeit, Ausdauer und Planmässigkeit aufweisen, sondern den emotionalen Elementen gleich die polaren Gegensätze in kurzer Schwingungszeit durchlaufen, so dass auf Perioden gesteigerter, ungewöhnlicher Aktivität und Arbeitsfreude Zeiten gänzlicher Passivität und verzweifelten Nichtstuns folgen."

[9]During the *Symposium*, while this lecture was being delivered, somebody distributed an anonymous leaflet signed, "A Prophetic Voice of the People", demanding an election, "of our Patriarch Joseph I as the President of the Ukrainian State".

[10]M. Bradovych (pseud. of M. Trotskyi), *Odna natsiia - odna tserkva* (n. p., 1950).

[11]P. B. T. Bilaniuk, *Ukrains'ka Tserkva — ii suchasne i maibutnie* (Toronto-Chicago, 1966).

[12]On religion and religiosity of the Ukrainian people, cf. V. Mansikka, *Die Religion der Ostslaven* (Helsinki, 1922); V. Lypyns'kyi, *Relihiia i tserkva v istorii Ukrainy* (Philadelphia, 1935); M. Hrushevs'kyi, *Z istorii relihiinoi dumky na Ukraini* (2nd ed., Winnipeg–Munich–Detroit, 1962); S. Lesnoi, *Rus', otkuda ty? Osnovnye problemy istorii drevnei Rusi* (Winnipeg, 1964); *Metropolitan* Ilarion (Ohiienko), *Dokhrystiians'ki viruvannia ukrains'koho narodu* (Winnipeg, 1965); V. Ianiv, ed., *Relihiia v zhytti ukrains'koho narodu*; and G. P. Fedotov, *The Russian Religious Mind*, vol. I.

[13]O. Kul'tshyts'kyi ("National Characteristics of the Ukrainian People," p. 952), observes: "The center of the collective unconscious in the Ukrainian peasantry may be regarded as the eulogized image of the *magna Mater* — Mother Earth, the Demeter (Franko's* Mother Nature), who has the power to change the demons into comic little devils(Mirchuk)".

[14]Cf. *Pastyrs'kyi lyst vysokopreosviashchennishoho iepyskopa kyr Ivana Buchka, Apostol's'koho vizytatora ukraintsiv u Zakhidnii Evropi pro Katolyts'ku Aktsiiu* (n. p., 1952. It is dated: Dec. 22, 1951). In this "Pas-

toral Letter" the prevailing contemporary ideas and ideals concerning Ukrainian lay organizations are spelled out.

[15]The outstanding publication of this period was: *First Victims of Communism. White Book on the Religious Persecution in Ukraine. (Translated from the Italian)* (Rome, 1953). It was published also in: Italian, German, Spanish, French, and Ukrainian.

[16]For a complete list of organizations, cf. M. H. Marunchak, *The Ukrainian Canadians: A History* (Winnipeg-Ottawa, 1970), pp. 755-758, and *passim*.

[17]A. Senyshyn, "Ukrainians in the U. S.", *New Catholic Encyclopedia*, vol. 14 (New York, etc., 1967), pp. 375-376.

[18]On the traditional role of the Church Brotherhoods in Ukraine, cf. M. Hrushevs'kyi, *Istoriia Ukrainy-Rusy*, t. VI (Kiev-L'viv, 1907; reprinted by Knyho-Spilka, New York, 1955), pp. 412-663; and Ia. D. Isaievych, *Bratstva ta ikh rol' v rozvytku ukrains'koi kul'tury XVI-XVIII st.* (Kiev, 1966).

[19]See *Statut Mariis'koi Druzhyny* (n. p., n. d.). It was approved by Rev. N. Voiakovs'kyi, the Apostolic Visitor and Administrator for the Catholic Ukrainians in Germany, on March 5, 1947. The §17 (p. 10) reads: "The [spiritual] leader is the superior and director of the Sodality [of the Immaculate Conception of the Most Holy Virgin Mary]. Without his express or tacit approval no decision of the Council can have binding power. Decisions and elections performed in his absence become binding only after his additional confirmation". Even greater and broader are the prerogatives of the "Spiritual Caretaker" of the Ukrainian Catholic Brotherhood in Canada. Cf. *Statut Bratstva Ukraintsiv Katolykiv Kanady* (Toronto, 1957), §8-10 (pp. 5-6). The rights of "spiritual assistants" are mentioned in §34 (pp. 21-22).

[20]V. Ianiv, ed., *Ukrains'kyi myrianyn v zhytti tserkvy, spil'noty ta liudstva. Materiialy Studiinykh dniv UKhR (Rocca di Papa, 13-16 zhovtnia, 1963)* (Paris-Rome, 1966).

[21]*Chuzhynets' v oboroni Ukrains'koi Tserkvy* (Toronto, 1966). Reverend Clayton Barclay died in the summer of 1974. He was a priest of the newly created Ukrainian Catholic Eparchy of New Westminster, B. C., Canada.

[22]Prof. Bohdan Popel became the first head of the Central Committee and remained in office until his death on January 1, 1971. His prudence, wisdom, and strong character were a source of inspiration for Ukrainian Catholic laity in their confrontations with the hierarchy. Prof. Popel was succeeded by Hryhorii Holovatyi from Toronto.

[23]The impetus for organizing the Society for the Promotion of the Patriarchal System in the Ukrainian Catholic Church was provided by Professor Mykola Chubatyj (1889-1975) in his series of articles entitled "Sprava Kyivs'koho Patriiarkhatu ta maibutnie nashoho khrystiianstva," published in *Amerika* (Philadelphia), June 5-7, 1964. Soon thereafter the Committee for the Patriarchate was created under the chairmanship of Bohdan Shebunchak, M.D. The first convention of delegates and representatives from various local committees in the U.S. met in New York on June 19, 1965, drew up bylaws and elected Wasyl Pasiczniak (currently the editor of the Society's journal *Za Patriiarkhat*) president of the Society. The second convention, held in 1968, elected Wasyl Kaczmar of Newark presi-

dent. He was followed by Zenovij Gill, M.D. of Trenton, who was elected in 1970, and by Myroslaw Nawrockyj, M.D. of Philadelphia (elected in 1972). The Society also established a Council of Laity. It was headed in succession by Roman Osinchuk, M.D., Miroslav Labunka, Ph.D., and Roman Danylewycz. The initial goal of the Society was to induce the Vatican to recognize the Kyiv-Halych Metropolia as a patriarchate and to install the Confessor of Faith Josyf Slipyj as the first patriarch. However, because of strong opposition by the Vatican Curia and principally by the S. Congregation for the Eastern Churches, the Society has developed a far-ranging program for the defense of the rights of the Autonomous Ukrainian Catholic Church and for the eventual culmination of her organizational structure in a patriarchate. In addition to lobbying and writing letters and petitions to Pope Paul VI and to Ukrainian and Latin rite hierarchy, the Society has staged several demonstrations and called several press conferences both in the U.S. and in Europe with the intent to dramatize the plight of the Ukrainian Catholic Church. These activities of the Society have been widely reported by the news media.

[24]Cf. "Informatsii pro pratsiu Svitovoho Tovarystva za Patriiarkhal'nyi Ustrii Ukrains'koi Katolyts'koi Tserkvy," dated June, 1974, and signed by Volodymyr Pushkar, President, and Daria Kuzyk, Secretary. Over the period of five years these two people worked assiduously to organize patriarchal movement in various countries of the world. Without their efforts The Ukrainian Patriarchal World Federation would not have materialized. At this time I would like to express my gratitude to Mrs. Kuzyk for supplying me with valuable source-materials for this paper.

[25]On June 3, 1973, a new organization, the Inter-Country Coordinating Centre of Ecclesial, Lay and Civic Organizations for Autonomy and Patriarchate of the Ukrainian Catholic Church was founded in Toronto, Ontario, and headed by Julian Pelech. Vasyl Markus was elected Secretary pro tem. Cf. *Biuleten'* Mizhkraiovoho Koordynatsiinoho Oseredku Tserkovno-Myrians'kykh i Hromads'kykh Organizatsii za Pomisnist' i Patriiarkhat UKTserkvy, No. 1 (Toronto-Chicago, 31 August, 1973). On p. 14, this organization calls itself the "Provisional Supreme Council of Laity" ("Tymchasova Holovna Rada Myrian").

[26]For the text of Eugene Cardinal Tisserant's letter, see *Svoboda* (Jersey City), Oct. 10, 1970, and *Za Patriiarkhat*, rik IV, ch. 3 (14) (Oct. 1970), p. 24. The letter was addressed to Dr. Mary Klachko of New York in response to her letter sent to the Cardinal with the booklet: " . . . *And Bless Thine Inheritance*" by Eva Piddubcheshen ([Schenectady, N.Y., 1970]).

*Ivan Franko (1856-1916) - a noted Ukrainian poet and scholar.

Index of

Biblical References:

index of names:

Shebunchak, B. 172
Sheptyts'kyj A. (Metro-
    politan) see Szeptycky
Shlemkevych, M. 170
Shook, L.K. 40
Sikorskii, V. 170
Simeon the New Theologian
    60
Sinai 25
Singh Kirpal 4
Siricius, Pope, 109, 117,
    118
Skovoroda, H. 143
Slipyj, J. (Patriarch) 54
    164, 167, 173
Smulders, P. 84, 89, 90, 92
Socrates 106, 107, 111, 148
Soiron Th. 3
Sozomenos 107
Spyridonos 107
Staniloae, D. 12
Steinthal, H. 169
Stoop, J.A.A. 62
Strucker, A. 50
Synesius 111
Synge, F.C. 39
Szeptyćky, A. (Metro-
    politan) 45,.128

Tabachnykov, I.A. 152
Teilhard de Chardin, Pierre
    (S.J.) 20, 21, 41, 47, 71
Tertullian 5, 50, 62, 72
Thabor 25, 27, 28
Theodoret 59, 108
Theodorou, A. 61
Theodosius 110
Theophilos of Antioch 56
Thomas Aquinas, St. (O.P.)
    62
Thurian, M. 136
Tisserant, E. (Cardinal)
    163, 165, 168, 173
Todd, J.M. 171
Tower of Babel 36
Trembelas, P. 61
Tresmontant, C. 74, 83
Trotskyi, M. 171
Tsehel's'kyi, L. 169
Tsymbalistyi, B. 170
Tychyna, P. 153
Tyciak, J. 105

Urban VIII, Pope 122

Vacandarol, E. 104
Vailhe, S. 40
Valerga, G. (Latin rite
    Patriarch) 125
Van Ackeren, G.F. 154
Vann, Gerald (O.P.) 41
Velykyi, A.H. 170
Vinch, J. de (also Vinck)
    13, 41
Voiakovs'kyi, N. 172
Vorgrimler, H. 64, 65, 90,
    138, 154
Vosté, J.M. 39
Vovk, K.H. 170
Vries, W. de 120, 124, 126,
    134

Waal, A. de 40, 41
Walland, F. 62
Wand, J.W.C. 40
Weber, L.M. 131
Wikenhauser, A. 52
Wild, Ph. T 62
Wilmart, D.A. 39
Witley, W.T. 62
Wulf, F. 3
Wulff, O. 40

Yutang, Lin 48

Zaehner, R.C. 51
Zankow, S. 61
Ziegler, J.G. 131
Zielinski, B. 39
Ziesler, J.A. 39

index:

rite, synod (1274) 137
ecclesial legislation 130
ecclesiastical decency 125
ecclesiasticism 67
ecclesiology 52
    ideology 161
ecstatic union 57
ecumenical
    dialogue 161
    spirit 100, 102
Edict of Milan (313) 106
Egypt 111
    ancient 48
Elvira, synod of 106, 109,
    118
emanation, intellectual 94
Emmanuel 67
emotion 29
enanthropesis 61
encratic tendencies 57, 109
energetics of love 20
entropy 26
Eo quamvis tempore 123
eparchy 168
epiclesis 37, 45
Epiphany 78
eternity 94
epopteia 49
eschatology
    community 47
    eschata 23, 28, 66
    fulfillment 47
    question 25
    realized 27, 55, 64, 65
esoteric knowledge 49
eternal life 54, 66
ethics 145
ethnarch 160
ethnopsychology 157
ethos 157
Etsi pastoralis 124
Eucharist 52, 54, 148
    Eucharistic presence 33
evil 46
evolution 20, 26, 79, 82
    convergence 74
    homogenous 74
    irreversibility 74
    universal 80
exaggerated individualism
    159
existence, pure 77
existential Philosophy 83
experience, personal 85

religious 32

faith 65, 145
fall of man 51
    biological evolution 51
    original sin 51
    primordial dragon 51
    serpent 51
    titanism 51
Family, Divine 14
Fathers of the Church 147
    148
feeling 29
Filioque 45
firstborn 31
Florence, Council of (1438-
    1439) 122
forgiveness of sins 122
formal object 90
"forward, human" 80
freedom 74, 94, 169
fulfillment of the world 26
fundamental sciences 145

Gangres, Council of 106
glorification of man 61, 62
glory 23, 25, 26, 27, 28,
    37, 53, 55, 169
gnosis 57
    hermetic 49
Gnosticism 49, 55, 56, 57,
    104
God 30, 75, 145
    Giver of grace 145
    hyper-immanent 30
    Kingdom of 32, 33, 35,
    66, 79, 138, 147, 149
    liberty of 90
    motive 89
    para-immanent 30, 78
    trans-immanent 30, 78
    union with creation 91
God the Father 9, 10, 14,
    24, 31, 32, 91, 105
God-man 23, 24, 59, 88, 89
goodness 38
grace, divine 37, 46, 62,
    76, 150
    adoption 62
    gratuity of 93
Great Mother 162
Greece 111
Greek Fathers 55, 59
Greek legislation 123

81, 88, 95, 145
papocaesarism 67
Parousia 28, 33, 80, 89
patriarch 160, 169
patriarchal society 169
patriarchate 169
Patriarchate of Moscow 168
patriiarkhal'nyky 166
patrimony 160
patriotism 153
patristic tradition 105
    piety 60
Paul, St. 103
Pavia, Synod of (1081) 110
Pax Romana 162
Pelagianism 67
Pentecost 23
people of God 34, 51
person 23, 29, 32, 35, 50,
    67, 145
personalist philosophy 35
personalized universe 64
pessimism 63, 67
pharaoh 48
philosophy 144, 145
    of religion 146
    of the heart 143, 148
piety 109
Platonism 49, 83
Pleroma 49, 79, 81, 92, 95
pneumatics 56
Pneumatophor 10, 36, 47, 55
Pneumatology 47
poets 29
Poltava 144
polylogue 11
Pontifical Ukrainian Col-
    lege of St Josaphat in
    Rome 163
popes 102, 120, 139
postulant, unmarried 113
Powers 31
pravda 81
prayer 3-14, 32, 50
    adoration 7
    and the Fathers of the
    Church 4
    answer 9
    charism of the Holy
    Spirit 4
    definitions 4
    description 5, 14
    dialogue 4
    divine initiative and

    condescension 5
    efficient causality of
    4
    gift of Triadic God 7
    glorification 7
    imploration 7
    interfaith polylogue 7
    monologue 4
    natural 5
    Pelagian sense 4
    pneumatological view 14
    polylogue 5, 12, 14, 19
    primitive form 5
    public cult 5
    supernatural act 4
    supernatural reality 5
predestination 63
presbyters 112
priest 115
    remarriage 115
    wives of 110, 138
primus motor immobilis 90
Principalities 31
prophets 24, 51, 66
Protestant Church 136
    ecclesial groups 161
Providence Association 164
psychic center 85
psycho-somatic unity 29
psychology 76
purgatory 45
purity of heart 148

Qua sollerti 127
Quinisext in Trullo 114
Qumram 52

rationalism 76
reality, salvational 145
    super-rational 145
recapitulation 56
reconciliation 91
redemption 37, 56, 62, 75,
    92, 93, 94
reformata semper reformanda
    35
regeneration 26, 62
religion 83, 143
    agape-type 162
    eros-type 161
    nomos-type 162
    phobos-type 162
religious indifferentism 67
religious pluralism 161

religious profession 111
remoteness, religious 91
   ethical 91
re-mythologization 64
reparation 62
research, scholarly 143
responsibility, moral 50
Resurrection 25, 27, 28, 46
   62, 88
revelation 83
   word-revelation 145
   work-revelation 145
revolution 64
Roman Apostolic See 163
Roman Curia 120, 124, 126,
   127, 165, 167
Roman Empire 106
Roman liturgy 117
Roman Prima Primaria 162
Roman primacy 45
Roman Synod of 386 109
Rome 114
Rumanian archbishop 125
Russian language 81

Sacerdotalis Caelibatus
   119, 129
sacralism, exaggerated 67
sacramentalism 67
sacramentals 34
Sacraments 34, 54, 66
Sacred Congregation for the
   Propagation of the Faith
   122, 125, 127
sacred languages 147
sacred virginity 131
   devaluation of 136
   element of Christian
   unity 136
   monastic life 136
salvation 62
   history of 22, 23, 24,
   33
sanctification 62, 63, 103
   150
scholarly dialogue 89
scholastic philosophy 87
scholastic theology 87
scientists 29
Scotist school 91, 92, 93
Scriptures, Holy 103
second death 38
secularization 67
self-knowledge 144

self-love, necessary 95
self-revelation, divine
   145
self-transcendence 30, 65,
   77
semeion 33
separation of Church and
   state 60
sexuality 105
Shevchenko Scientific
   Society 63
Sikhism 48
sin 38, 46, 62, 90, 95
Sinai 22
slavery 110
Society for the Promotion
   of the Patriarchal
   System in the Ukrainian
   Catholic Church 166
Sodality of Our Lady 162,
   164
solemn magisterium 88
Son of God 14, 24, 93, 94,
   105
Son of Man 24, 26, 33, 88
sonship, divine 52
sophia 75
soteriology 49, 52
soul 31
Soviet Russian armed force:
   158
Soviet scholarship 143
spirit, incarnate 28
spiritual assistant 164
spirituality 60
   mystical 37
spiritualization 61
stability 80
Stoicism 49, 151
subdeacons 113
substance 31
Super-Humanité, Super-
   Christ, Super-Charité
   21
supernatural act of faith
   148
supernatural gift 148
supernatural order 76
Supreme Being 145
synergism 4
Synoptic Gospels 53
synthesis, theological 93
Syrian Catholic Synod of
   Sarfeh (1888) 126

TABLE OF CONTENTS: